Securing an Internship in the Sport Industry:

Promoting Your Professional Brand in Your Application Materials, Networking Opportunities, & Interviews

Kelli J. Donahue

Second Paperback Edition

University of Michigan

Ann Arbor, MI 48109

This book is intended for Michigan Sport Management students enrolled in SM 217: Business Communications.

As the creator and instructor of this course, and an internship advisor/career counselor in the Sport Management Program for over ten years, I've assisted hundreds of students with their internship and full-time job searches. The advice in this book is based on the experiences and successes of our SM graduates, as well as advice from numerous sport industry employers. Thank you to all contributors for sharing your stories with me and for being willing and supportive mentors for all of our talented SM students.

A special thanks to Ostap Rapeyko, SM Class of 2015, for your thoughtful editing and suggestions. Go Blue!

Chapter 1

Beginning Your Internship Search

Chapter 1   Beginning Your Internship Search

Searching for an internship can be a lengthy process requiring time, effort, and diligence. There are resources on campus and within the School of Kinesiology to assist you; however, to maximize your efforts you'll also need to pursue leads on your own and build your professional network. The best time to start this process is now. The information in this chapter will help you get started with your research and preparation phase.

Identify Your Areas of Interest

An internship is an opportunity for you to gain professional skills and experience while also assessing whether or not a specific area of the industry is a good fit for you. Many students enter the Sport Management Program with intentions of working in a particular area of the industry like marketing, team operations, or sponsorship. After exposure to other areas of the industry through internship experiences, job shadows, and guest speaker presentations, many of these same students change their minds. Exposure to diverse experiences and the resulting revision of career plans is a natural occurrence, part of your undergraduate education, and one of the many benefits of a Michigan education.

As a Sport Management student, you'll be exposed to faculty, alumni, and industry executives through your coursework, guest speaker presentations, career fairs, and networking events. You should take advantage of every opportunity to learn about the industry and meet professionals from different organizations and positions. In addition, you should be reading and staying informed of current events. *The Sport Business Journal* (*SBJ*) is the lead publication for sport industry business news. I strongly encourage you to purchase a subscription and make this journal part of your daily reading (it's required for my Business Communications course and the junior/senior-level Career Planning course). *SBJ* provides a student discount – information will be provided on your course syllabus or via an announcement. In addition, you should be reading other business publications, including the *Harvard Business Review, Forbes*, etc., and following industry organizations and leaders on social media.

As you begin to identify organizations and positions that interest you, keep in mind that you should aim to diversify your experiences. Again, like many of our freshmen and sophomore-level students, you may think you want to work in a certain area now, but there is great value in experiencing diverse areas so that you have a broader view of potential opportunities. We've also received feedback from numerous employers that students with diverse skills and experiences are more attractive candidates for employment. A diverse resume shows an employer that you are capable of handling a range of responsibilities and learning new skills and content.

Once you begin to identify organizations that interest you, you'll need to conduct a great deal of research on each organization and organize your information in a master database for future use. I strongly suggest creating a Google spreadsheet. In fact, I suggest it so strongly that it's a requirement of my junior/senior-level Career Planning course. If you feel so inclined, and you'd like to better prepare yourself for your internship search and build your network, start building your database now. All the cool kids are doing it.

Your spreadsheet should include the following information on each organization:

- Name of organization
- Locations – particularly address of location that interests you
- Internship positions available and application process details, including due date and required application materials
- Names of employees in the organization who you would like to contact and their contact information (If there is a Michigan alumni there, highlight this contact's name and information)
- Date of your first contact with someone in the organization and then continuing contact dates and details
- Current hot topics/business news regarding this organization to use as talking points during an informative or formal interview

This spreadsheet is going to be one of your best resources as you search for internships and eventually for full-time jobs upon graduation. In the past five years, almost all of the Sport Management students who have created their own master databases have secured full-time jobs within a month of graduation. It also greatly reduces anxiety as these students have felt more prepared, focused, and confident in their progress towards securing employment.

Ideally, you are adding to this spreadsheet continuously throughout your undergraduate years. The more contacts you add and the more extensive your information on each organization, the stronger and broader your network will be. Then, remember, it's not enough to simply record people's contact information - you must make contact with these employers. This should be a continuous process, not just one email message. We'll discuss relationship networking further in Chapter 5: Promoting Your Brand & Building Your Network.

School of Kinesiology, Campus, & On-line Career Resources

Kinesiology Resources

The School of Kinesiology will provide you with numerous opportunities to meet and network with industry professionals. These opportunities will be provided through in-class and out-of-class guest speaker presentations, career fairs, and alumni networking events. In addition, our two leading student organizations, the Sport Business Association (SBA) and the Michigan Sport Business Conference (MSBC), will host networking and professional development activities. You should take advantage of all of these opportunities. In addition, find time to speak with your Sport Management faculty and staff about your career plans. Your faculty and staff, such as your faculty mentor and academic advisor, can help you assess potential career paths and suggest potential employers or contacts. The Kinesiology Office of Undergraduate Student Affairs (OUSA) also purchases an updated copy of the *Sports Market Place Directory*, which includes sport industry employers categorized both by geographic location and area of the industry. This book may be checked out and reviewed in the OUSA.

Michigan Career Center
As a Michigan student, you also have access to the Michigan Career Center located in the Student Activities Building (SAB). The Career Center is an excellent resource for all things related to your internship search, including career advising, resume/cover letter reviews, and mock interviewing. The Career Center's professional staff members take appointments and peer advisors see students on a walk-in basis. You should make a point of checking out the Career Center's website (careercenter.umich.edu) weekly to take advantage of upcoming workshops, presentations, career fairs, and other events that may be

helpful to you. The Career Center also has a link to the "Career Center Connector" where you will find internship and job postings.

Michigan Alumni Association
With more than 535,000 living Maize & Blue alumni, the Michigan network is an excellent resource. The Alumni Association actively hosts networking and career coaching events to assist students and alumni in their ongoing job searches. In addition to checking the Career Center's site weekly, you should also check the alumni association's site to stay informed of upcoming opportunities.

LinkedIn
With over 300 million members, LinkedIn is a useful business site that facilitates networking and job searches. More than 190,000 U-M alumni are on LinkedIn, so it's an excellent resource to connect with them as well. Your LinkedIn profile should include your relevant education and internship experiences; you may also include your career objectives. Consider it your personal, professional site. It should be used to connect with industry professionals and facilitate career networking, which we will discuss further in Chapter 5. Employers often post open jobs and recruit top candidates via LinkedIn. In fact, we're hearing from more students each year who are directly contacted by employers via the site.

Your LinkedIn profile should be updated frequently and you should be connecting with business professionals as much as possible. We'll discuss your active use of LinkedIn, building your profile and making connections, in class and in Chapter 5.

Teamwork Online

Teamwork Online (teamworkonline.com) was developed as an extension of Teamwork Consulting in 2000. The site is a full service, job search site. Employers post open positions and candidates may apply via the site.

You're encouraged to set up your Teamwork Online profile as soon as possible and begin browsing the site. The videos of industry employers are helpful and informative, as are the updates and testimonials. The site offers 50 free business cards to students (with a small shipping fee), and it hosts networking events throughout the year. Many of our students have had success finding internships via Teamwork Online. It shouldn't be your only job search tool, but it is a valuable complement to the other resources included in this chapter to broaden and increase the success of your internship search.

Factors to Consider When Searching for an Internship

Now that you have some information to help you research prospective employers and build your network of industry contacts in your master database, you can begin narrowing and focusing your search by choosing those organizations you will apply to first. Remember, there's great value in gaining diverse experiences, so while you may be targeting a specific industry area or even a specific organization, you're advised to expand your search to include additional organizations and types of internships. This will broaden your experiences and improve your likelihood of receiving an offer.

As you're applying to internships, there are a number of factors you'll need to consider to ensure you're focusing your search strategically to best meet your individual needs and circumstances:

Your Current Experience/Year in School
To some degree, the type of organization or internship position to which you apply will be dependent on your previous experience and your year in school. Considering you're a sophomore-level student enrolled in SM 217, you may not have held a relevant sport internship yet. So, while you may target professional teams or the major leagues, you should definitely target "smaller" organizations as well, like minor league teams and leagues, smaller marketing firms, etc. Many of the established, formal internship programs of larger organizations

will require students to have gained previous internship experience and be of rising junior standing. First and second-year students generally have greater success securing an internship in the minor leagues, smaller firms, or outside of the "Big Four" sports.

Is the Internship Paid or Unpaid? If Unpaid, Can You Afford it?
Most internship employers pay their interns either in monetary payment or in the form of class credits, though the two are not mutually exclusive. Some employers require that students be registered for academic credits in order to complete the internship, some may provide an hourly wage or stipend, and some employers will provide the opportunity to receive both monetary payment and class credits.

If you are required to, or interested in, receiving academic credits for your internship experience, please review the SM 403 paperwork. You will need to register and pay for the credit hours.

Do You Have (or Can You Find) Housing in the Area?
If you're fortunate enough to live in or near an industry-rich city or town, this may be an ideal situation as you can live at home with your parents while working. If, however, you aren't able to live at home and commute to work, or you don't secure an internship in or near your hometown, you may be able to secure alternative free or affordable housing. Some internship employers will provide free housing for the

intern staff, in which case, this detail is generally provided in the internship posting. If housing isn't provided and your financial situation will allow it, you can look into subletting an apartment for the duration of your internship, renting a room, or possibly staying in a local university's housing (many colleges open their dormitories to summer interns, for a fee). This could also be a good time to call that distant aunt and uncle and ask to live with them for a summer.

Timing of the Internship and Required Hours
Internships will vary in their duration, as well as start and end dates. Many of the established organizations' formal internship programs will last eight weeks. Sometimes you will be asked to rank your preference and then be assigned to either the first eight weeks or the second eight weeks of the summer months. On the other hand, most baseball teams will want you to start immediately after your spring classes conclude and stay for the duration of the summer. Sometimes these details are disclosed in the job posting and other times they do not become known until the interview.

As you are applying, consider your own availability and be aware that while some employers may be flexible with your dates of employment, most will expect you to adhere to their needs. In addition, particularly if you are working for a team, you'll find that the hours posted are not necessarily the hours you'll work. It's fairly routine for employers to post 40 hours/week; yet, you may find yourself regularly working 50+ hours weekly.

It's not advisable to ask how many hours you can expect to work each week during the interview process unless you absolutely must know in order to make additional plans (for example, perhaps you must know because you also must hold a part-time, paid position to make ends meet). It's best, if your situation allows, to assume you'll be working long hours.

Employers' Timeline: Accepting Applications and Extending Offers
You'll quickly find that all employers follow their own timeline in the internship search process. Some sport industry employers, such as the NBA league offices, will generally post their summer internship opportunities and require materials to be submitted for consideration in the late fall preceding the summer in which you would work. Other employers will post internship opportunities as late as April and May and expect you to start that June. Others may never post their opportunities at all, which does not mean they will not take on an intern. In this case, you should call an employer and ask to speak with someone about the possibility of interning.

For your planning purposes, you should include in your internship master database the dates you can expect employers to post internship opportunities and their application deadlines. If you're looking for a summer internship, your search process should begin the preceding fall and may last until the following spring.

You'll also find that the amount of time that passes from when you first apply to a position to when you are first contacted by an employer will vary. In addition, you may interview once, twice, or three or four times with the same employer before being extended an offer or declined from further consideration (the interviewing process will be discussed further in Chapter 6). Since each employer's timeline will vary, you'll want to continue applying to positions throughout the fall, winter, and spring months until you have secured an internship.

Securing an internship can seem like a daunting task; however, if you start your application process early, strategically make use of our campus resources and your professional network, and dedicate time to preparing and seeking reviews of your application materials and interviewing skills, you can expect to achieve success. The following chapters will discuss the preparation of your internship application materials: your resume, cover letter, and potential additional materials.

In Summary:

1. Start your internship search process now.

2. Build a master database of industry employers and internship information.

3. Make use of available resources:

    a. Campus resources like your academic advisor, faculty mentor, the Michigan Alumni Center, and the Michigan Career Center

    b. Your personal and professional network: family, friends, former employers, and your Michigan faculty and staff

    c. On-line resources like organization websites, LinkedIn, and Teamwork Online

4. Expect each employer's internship application process to be different in the requirements and the timing/length of the process.

5. Consider your personal financial and housing options, and your career development plan as you search for internships.

Chapter 2

Preparing Your Resume

Chapter 2 Preparing Your Resume

Applying for an internship is a sales process. You have to sell your professional skills to an employer and persuade her/him that you're the most qualified applicant. To accomplish this, it's important that your application materials portray you in the most persuasive, and professional, way possible. In these next few chapters, we'll focus on developing your application materials: your resume, cover letter, references, recommendation letters, and possible portfolio materials. This chapter will focus specifically on preparing your resume.

Your resume is an informative document with persuasive appeal. Employers look to your resume to evaluate your educational background, experiences, and skills as they relate to the position to which you have applied. *Most employers will spend less than one minute scanning your resume.* Based on this scan, your resume may be placed in the potential-interview pile, the save-for-review-later pile, or the discard pile. You obviously want to be placed in the potential-interview pile. This may be the hardest part of the application process - simply getting chosen for an interview from what may be a pile of hundreds or thousands of other qualified candidates. You can increase your chances greatly by spending time on preparing a professional resume that is easy to read, well organized, and cleanly formatted.

The content of your resume must reflect factual, accurate information. This means you have to work with the experiences you have gained so far. If you're a first or second year student, you may be light on experience. One of your main goals during your undergraduate education is to continue adding to and diversifying your experiences, so that you can strengthen your qualifications, and thus, the content of your resume.

If you're preparing your resume for the first time, it's helpful to start by brainstorming and listing experiences that you think are relevant to include. From this list, you can then determine the organization of your resume and the headers that best represent your experiences. "Relevant" experiences are those that demonstrate job-related skills, like organizational, leadership, communication, and teamwork skills, work ethic, etc. Employers in the sport industry will want to see sport-relevant experience on your resume. If you have yet to work for a sport organization, think of other positions that you've held that will show these relevant skills.

Organizing Your Resume
Employers won't spend time reading or scanning resumes that don't look good. Appearance absolutely matters. Your resume should be formatted clearly, easy to read, make use of proper spacing and white

space, and be free of typos. The headers of your resume should reflect your most relevant experiences in decreasing order of importance and you should format your content so that the most important information stands out in a quick scan.

General Rules to Follow

As you prepare your resume, follow these formatting guidelines:

- Stick to one page. You may go beyond one page after graduation, once you've held a professional position or positions for many years.

- Make it easy to read. Size 12 font is recommended; you may use 11 point if absolutely necessary (employers don't feel great about resumes that make them feel like their eye sight is going). Use two to three font styles max and use them consistently (one for headers, one for descriptive text, and one for your name).

- Make use of white space with clean and consistent spacing and uniform margins; a .5-inch to a one-inch margin is acceptable.

- Start with "Education" as your first header. Employers will expect to see education first as you're still a student. After you've graduated and worked for a year, move education below your experience header.

- Use bold-faced font and italics sparingly to make your most important information stand out.

- Be consistent in your formatting. This adds unity to your design and visual appeal. It also makes important information easier to find.

Use of Headers

The headers you use will be dependent on the content you're including on your resume. For this reason, your headers may be different from one of your peer's resume's headers; no two resumes will be, or should be, exactly the same. You want your resume to reflect your personal, professional skills.

As a general rule, each header should have at least two entries beneath it (positions/jobs), except for "Education," which can have only one entry. Headers you may show on your resume include:

Education – At this time, this is your first header. It should include the University of Michigan directly beneath it, preferably in bold-faced font, with your major and graduation year. You may also include overseas study under this header, U-M affiliated clubs/organizations, and possibly your high school (we will discuss when to include your high school in class).

Internship Experience – This header is recommended if you have at least two relevant internship experiences to include.

Experience – This is a common header for first and second-level undergraduate students as you most likely haven't held two internship experiences yet. "Experience" is a general header under which you can include paid, unpaid, internship, volunteer, and leadership positions.

Leadership Experience – This header should only be used if you've held office in at least two relevant clubs or organizations. It shouldn't be used for general membership.

Additional Qualifications or *Skills* – It's common to include a final header that lists other relevant experiences or skills. This header may include other positions that are relevant, but which you did not have space to include with bulleted descriptions beneath your main experience header. It may also include skills, such as software skills (beyond MS Office), social media skills, editing skills, second language proficiency, etc. Junior and senior-level students generally don't have room for this header; it can be a helpful and relevant space filler for younger students who don't have extensive internship experience.

I often see an "Activities" header on high school students' resumes. "Activities" is not recommended as a header beyond high school as this generally includes hobbies and other such experiences that are no longer considered relevant. If you're including your high school under "Education" (it would go beneath "University of Michigan"), you may still include things like, "Captain, Varsity Soccer," if you have the space. High school activities are appropriate to include if you're a first or second-level undergraduate student, though they should be deleted and replaced with content reflecting your college experiences and professional positions as soon as possible.

Choosing Your Resume Layout & Design

When choosing your overall resume design and layout - meaning the headers you will include, placement of content, and spacing - consider how much content you have to include. Some design layouts lend themselves to using white space and line spacing well for those with a lot of content, and others make use of white space and spacing well to extend limited content to fill the entire page. The example resumes at the end of this chapter make use of design layouts that work well for most sophomore to senior-level students. Additional resume examples are posted to our ctools page under "Resources," as well as to the Career Center's website.

Your Content: Organizing and Describing Your Experiences

As you'll see in the resume examples provided at the end of this chapter, it's important that your resume's content reflect your experiences in quick, easy-to-read wording that reads clearly and with confidence. Your experiences/positions should be organized in reverse-chronological order. This means you'll list any currently held positions first and then list your other experiences by going backward in time.

Bulleted descriptions read quickly; paragraph descriptions do not. For this reason, bulleted descriptions are highly recommended and should really be considered the standard. You should include a minimum of two bullets for each entry and a maximum of six bullets. The number of bullets you include should reflect the significance of the position; for example, if it was a very relevant position in which you held great responsibility and worked on a number of projects, you should include four to six bullets. On the other hand, if the position did not involve as much responsibility you should only include two bullets.

Experiences with a greater number of bullets will draw an employer's eye even if they end up being further down the page (remember, positions are listed in reverse-chronological order based on when the position was held). So, including a greater number of bullets is an effective way to make relevant positions stand.

Current positions should be written in present tense while past positions should be written in past tense. Your bulleted descriptions should reflect what you did, the responsibilities you held in your internship, the projects you worked on *and* the outcomes of your work. If you're able to include tangible information (e.g.: the number of fans who attended your event or the percent increase in social media followers as a result of your work), you should do so.

Each bulleted description should start with a verb. Verbs read with confidence and action. You should add variety and interest to your resume by varying the verbs you use. Ideally, each individual organization/position entry's bullets begin with a different verb. It's even more ideal (though difficult) to begin every bulleted description on the resume with a different verb. The sample resumes at the end of this chapter demonstrate this.

The Michigan Career Center's on-line resources include a list of relevant resume action verbs. The Career Center also includes additional resume writing tips and sample resumes. All can be found on the Career Center's website at: careercenter.umich.edu

Having Your Resume Reviewed
It 's very important that you have a number of people review your resume and give you feedback prior to you sending it out to employers. Your reviewers will help you find typos you missed, tweak

wording, or revise content. Most likely, each reviewer will give you slightly different feedback, which is excellent. You can then take each person's feedback and decide what works best for you based on your individual goals and preferences.

You may want to ask your parents or friends to review your resume. It's also recommended that you ask professionals in the field in which you intend to work, your faculty, academic advisor, or one of the professional staff in the Michigan Career Center. In addition, Sport Management Program alumni will make themselves available to conduct resume reviews and mock interviews at various times during the academic year. These opportunities will be announced via email from the School of Kinesiology Office of Undergraduate Student Affairs. The SBA board and MSBC board will also offer resume review opportunities with upperclassmen, alumni, and industry professionals.

Submitting Your Resume and Other Application Materials
When emailing an employer your application materials, attach your materials as PDFs rather than Word documents as PDFs maintain their integrity no matter what software program a person is using. Name each document with your full name and its title
(e.g.: KelliDonahueResume, KelliDonahueCoverLetter, etc.).

For the purpose of printing your resume, cover letter, and reference list, it's worth the investment to buy some quality card stock. By the point of your sophomore year, you should be carrying a few copies of your resume on you at all times. You never know when you may find yourself in an elevator with a potential employer (time to start rehearsing your elevator pitch, more on that later).

When assembling and snail mailing hard copies of your application materials to employers, your materials should be assembled with your cover letter first, followed by your resume, and then your reference list and any other materials you're including. You may also paperclip a business card to the top of your resume.

Snail mail your materials in a business envelope. Organize your materials in the order listed above and then trifold them all at once (fold the bottom third up first and then the top third down, so that the documents open with the top first). Then, stuff the envelope so that the front opening of your documents faces the back of the envelope.

Regular mail is an acceptable mailing method, though creativity can be beneficial, especially when applying to marketing or event management positions; for example, mailing your materials with express, over-night mail, will usually mean they skip the mail room and get dropped off directly on your contact's desk. Alternatively, you could mail your materials in a manila folder rather than a business envelope, which may help them stand out in the grouping of hundreds (if not thousands) of white business envelopes. Even more creative methods may be required for the more competitive internships. If you find yourself in need of creative ideas, tap into your network and ask for advice. Remember to gauge the position and the company. There's a time for creativity and a time to follow the standard methods, not all employers will require or appreciate totally out-of-the-box applications.

Sample Resumes

The following resume examples demonstrate the content, organization, and formatting suggestions discussed previously. As you'll see, each is different in the headers, content, and formatting used. Your resume doesn't have to look exactly like one of these resumes. They're provided as examples to guide you as you assemble your own resume. There are additional resume examples posted to our ctools page, as well as on the Michigan Career Center's site.

YOUR NAME

student@umich.edu   555-555-5555   43 Acorn Rd, Ann Arbor, MI 48109

EDUCATION
University of Michigan, Ann Arbor, MI
Bachelor of Arts Degree in Sport Management, Class of 2014
Member, Sport Business Association; *VP of Marketing*, Michigan Club Sports

EXPERIENCE
University of Michigan Athletic Department, Ann Arbor, MI
Marketing Intern   **September 2012 – Present**
- Create and implement unique promotional events for the University of Michigan Women's Basketball Program to attract a larger and more diverse fan base; Winter 2012 & 2013 promotional events resulted in a 5% and 4% increase in fan attendance at home games, respectively
- Conduct target market research via surveys and cold calls; summarize data; apply results to improve existing and create new marketing plans
- Execute all aspects of promotional events: contact and secure sponsors; set up and manage distribution of promotional materials; organize pre-game and half-time events and participants; breakdown and store materials following events

The M-Den, Ann Arbor, MI
Assistant Store Manager   **November 2012 –December 2013**
- Oversaw all facets of store operations including merchandising, store layout, product displays, and opening and closing procedures
- Managed staff of five employees: maintained employee schedules; trained and supervised staff in all aspects of customer service; ensured a quality experience for customers to improve store traffic and repeat business
- Voted Employee of the Month five times for exceeding sales expectations

Detroit Tigers, Detroit, MI
Merchandising Intern   **Summer 2013**
- Analyzed previous season's sales reports; designed 2013 season special merchandise based on previous top-selling items; resulted in 3% increase in sales
- Managed story inventory; submitted merchandise orders to ensure plentiful stock; designed window displays; created new point-of-purchase visual displays to attract customer traffic and improve sales volume
- Maintained store website; posted weekly specials and promotional giveaways

ADDITIONAL QUALIFICATIONS
Proficient in Google Applications, MS Office, Adobe Photoshop, and Social Media applications for promotional and marketing activities

THE STUDENT

53 My Road

Ann Arbor, MI 48109

student@umich.edu

555-555-5555

EDUCATION

University of Michigan, Ann Arbor, MI

Bachelor of Arts Degree in Sport Management Expected May 2014

Member, Sport Business Association

Queensland University, Queensland, Australia

Semester abroad, emphasis in marketing and accounting coursework, Winter 2013

INTERNSHIP EXPERIENCE

University of Michigan Sports Marketing Department, Ann Arbor, MI

Marketing Intern – Head Coach   September 2013 - Present

- Develop and execute game-day promotional events for revenue and non-revenue sports to increase fan attendance and improve game-day atmosphere
- Supervise team of five interns and delegate responsibilities for game-day event management to ensure smooth operations; prioritize tasks and make on-the-spot adjustments to problem solve and deal with staffing needs
- Create innovative strategies to appeal to each specific team's target demographic; succeeded in increasing ticket sales at Men's soccer and Women's basketball games
- Supervise development of promotional calendars for specific sports teams; schedule photography sessions and assemble materials for print; work with professional marketing staff to design promotional flyers using Adobe Photoshop

Beansters, Ann Arbor, MI

Barista   September 2012 - Present

- Work 15-20 hours/week while managing full academic course load
- Provide quality customer service with attention to special orders with speed and efficiency to encourage repeat business

Octagon Sports Marketing, Norwalk, CT

id8 Intern   Summer 2013

- Researched and developed marketing plans with fellow interns to leverage consumer/fan passion and attendance at Octagon's clients' events
- Proposed marketing initiatives to executives in bi-weekly presentations using MS PowerPoint; received positive feedback on communication skills and visuals
- Assisted in organization of office resources, including case studies, capabilities and final RFP responses and proposals; helped organize both paper and electronic files
- Assisted in organization of office resources, including case studies, capabilities and final RFP responses and proposals; helped organize both paper and electronic files

In Summary:

1. Applying to an internship is a sales process: you must sell your professional skills and competencies to an employer.

2. Prepare an easy-to-read, well organized, and clearly formatted one-page resume following the guidelines discussed in this chapter.

3. Ask multiple reviewers to give you feedback on your resume before sending it out.

4. Attach your application materials as PDFs to email messages.

5. Invest in quality card stock for printing hard copies of your application materials.

6. Start carrying around copies of your resume at all times in case you find yourself in a situation to ask for feedback or give your resume to an employer.

Chapter 3

Writing Your Cover Letters (yes, that's plural)

Chapter 3   Writing Your Cover Letters (yes, that's plural)

While you may be able to send the same version of your resume to multiple job postings, you'll need a unique cover letter for each position to which you apply. A resume is an informative document with persuasive appeal, but a cover letter is entirely a persuasive document. Its main purpose is to sell your skills and qualifications for the specific position you desire. For this reason, each cover letter should be revised to best sell your most relevant experiences to cater to each position's responsibilities.

As a side note, you'll most likely hear varying opinions about cover letters. It's true that some employers have said that while a cover letter is required, they don't spend much time (or any time) reading it. Yet, other employers have indicated that they won't even consider an applicant should their cover letter not be written well or include typos. Recent trends in social media and communication positions have resulted in some employers asking for "creative" cover letters or limiting text to very few words. In all cases, as was recommended for your resume, you should have multiple reviewers provide feedback on your cover letters prior to sending them out.

This chapter will focus on writing a standard, one-page cover letter. We'll discuss some more creative styles in class.

Gathering Information Before You Write

Read the Position Posting

Before writing a cover letter, you should gather information about the specific job responsibilities. Start by reading the job posting to find what the employer has indicated as desirable qualifications, as well as the position duties and responsibilities. You'll want to demonstrate your ability to handle these tasks in your cover letter.

As an example, consider an internship posting that is looking for candidates with strong communication skills and past experience in customer service. Determine which of your past experiences demonstrate these abilities. Then, include an example or examples from each experience and discuss how you used these skills, describing your experiences in further detail than what is listed on your resume.

A body paragraph of a cover letter for this posting could read:

> As a sales representative last summer for Dick's Sporting Goods, I attended two sales leadership workshops and participated in management training meetings. I applied the excellent customer service and sales skills I learned to provide

quality shopping experiences for our customers, earning "Top Monthly Associate" honors three times for exceeding my target sales goals. I honed my ability to communicate with diverse customers as I catered my sales approach based on each customer's needs. I am confident my customer service experience and my proven ability to exceed sales targets will make me a valuable intern with your sales team this summer.

In this example, the student mentioned past experiences that were relevant to the job posting and described these experiences with active voice and confident language. She does not simply say, "I have sales experience." She demonstrates her experience with a specific example, names the employer to give the experience credibility and draw attention to her resume description, describes her duties, and demonstrates how she achieved success in the position. The example she discussed was strategically chosen based on the desired skills listed in the job posting.

Talk to People Who Work(ed) There
In addition to reading the job posting, you should try to gather further information by speaking to any peers who have worked in this position or with this organization. You can also search for Michigan alumni who work(ed) for this organization via LinkedIn and reach out to them. Most Michigan alumni are happy to share information with you and this is an excellent way to build your network through relationship networking. You may also call into the organization's

human resources department and ask to conduct a brief informational interview to learn more about the organization's goals, the position's responsibilities, the organization's culture, and the skills needed to be successful in this position. All of this information will help you cater your cover letter and assist you in preparing should you be invited for an interview. We'll discuss interviewing preparation and strategies in our chapter on Interviewing *Successfully*.

If you speak to someone within the organization about the position, or were referred to the position by someone the employer works with or knows well, you should include this in your cover letter.

Organizing Your Cover Letter

A cover letter should be a one-page document. It should be clear, concise, well written, and focus on selling you for each position to which you apply. Standard cover letters include three to possibly five paragraphs organized with the following content.

Introduction: Paragraph 1

You should begin your cover letter with a standard business-letter greeting, preferably addressed to a specific person. If the job posting doesn't include a specific name, you should search on line or call into the organization to ask for the specific person who will be reviewing applications. One of my former students, Shannon Lynch (SM Class of 2015), was told by the Washington Nationals that she was interviewed because she went out of her way to find the social media supervisor's name on line. I'm sure her cover letter was also well written, but it clearly helped that Shannon demonstrated her competence, resourcefulness, and desire to obtain the social media position.

If you aren't able to find the application reviewer or supervisor's name, "Dear Internship Coordinator" or "Greetings Detroit Tigers Human Resources Representative" or something of that nature will work. "To Whom It May Concern" and "Dear Sir or Madam" are not recommended as they are generic and vague.

 The opening paragraph of your cover letter should introduce you and state the position to which you are applying. Then, you should refer to (or name drop) the person who referred you to apply to this position or shared information with you (if this is relevant and the employer knows of this person and respects/likes them). Next, include a preview sentence of your most relevant skills and/or experiences that qualify you for this position. These skills/experiences will be discussed in your cover letter's body paragraphs.

Body Paragraph(s): Paragraph 2, and Possibly 3 & 4

Following your introduction paragraph, you should include one to three body paragraphs that describe your qualifications. Again, the experiences and skills you choose to discuss should be chosen and described strategically so that you are responding to the position details listed in the job posting or those that you discovered through additional research. As you relate your experiences, name previous employers and your position titles when relevant to authenticate your experiences; detail your responsibilities, projects and/or specific actions; and then include tangible results to illustrate successful outcomes.

It's best to limit each body paragraph to one main thought. This may mean discussing one relevant skill and demonstrating it by describing two different experiences; or it may mean discussing one experience and the different skills that you gained through your work. Your body paragraphs should be concise, though detailed, and written following formal writing rules. Your descriptions should expand on those from your resume. Don't copy and paste the same wording from your resume to your cover letter. If you're including more than one body paragraph, organize them in decreasing order of importance (start with your most relevant experiences).

Closing Paragraph

Your final paragraph should close by summarizing your relevant skills, requesting to speak with the employer, and including your contact information. It can also be a benefit for Michigan students to include your availability to begin the internship; U-M's winter semester ends earlier than most schools, allowing you to begin an internship earlier than students from other colleges. Finally, you'll close with a standard business closing and your printed name. Leave space between your closing and your printed name for your signature.

Your signature and printed name may be followed by a closing similar to that of your email closing. We'll discuss email signatures further in class. They may include your school/major/graduation date and any current titles/positions you hold in relevant organizations. A sample email closing is provided below:

Sincerely,

Sara

Sarah Butler
VP Marketing, Sport Business Association
Sport Management Program
University of Michigan Class of 2015
sbutler@umich.edu   734-555-5555

Guidelines for Use of Language and Structure

As you write your cover letters, use active voice and confident language. Keep the tone positive and professional and follow formal writing rules:

- No contractions

- Left justify paragraphs, skip lines between paragraphs

- You can use the same header as included on your resume.

- Use active voice. This means many sentences will include "I" statements, but try to vary your language so not all sentences start with "I."

- Use positive language and tone. This is more of a subtle effect, though a beneficial one. Refrain from using "but," "however," "just," "simply," or other terms that may imply you are trying to spin something negative into a positive.

- Be confident. Refrain from using phrases like, "I believe," or "I think," and instead say "I am confident I will," or simply, "I will." An employer cannot trust you to fill a position if you don't sound confident and competent.

Sample Cover Letters

The following letters provide examples of content, wording organization, and formatting. More sample cover letters are provided on our ctools site, as well as on the Michigan Career Center site. Remember to have your cover letters edited by someone else before you send them out.

Student Name
555 Michigan Dr., Ann Arbor, MI 48190   student@umich.edu   555-555-5555

Ms. Lucia Lucern
Washington Kastles
509 7th Street NW
Washington, DC 20004

November 13, 2014

Dear Ms. Lucern:

I am interested in obtaining a media internship with the Washington Kastles in the summer of 2015. As a Sport Management major at the University of Michigan, I have studied the business of sport and gained relevant experience through my current and previous positions as a member of the Big Ten Network Student U Production Crew and as an intern with the Small/Medium Enterprise Group at Bank One. In each of these roles, I developed knowledge and skills that will make me a valuable addition to the Washington Kastles during the summer of 2015.

I am organized, responsible, and extremely dedicated. As a member of the Big Ten Network Student U Production Crew, I assist in producing video content of one to three Michigan athletic events per week. My work with this entirely student-run crew requires excellent time-management skills as I dedicate approximately fifteen hours per week to this position while successfully balancing my academic work.

During my time as an intern with Bank One, I was given the same responsibility as a professional staff member; for example, I was solely responsible for transferring the Small-Business Quarterly Newsletter into a live website. I took initiative to familiarize myself with Adobe Dreamweaver in order to create an end product that was up to both my standards, as well as the bank's standards. The website launch was successful and I received positive feedback from the bankers.

I would appreciate the opportunity to further discuss how my excellent leadership, communication and organizational skills, and my knowledge of athletic event video production will make me a valuable addition to the Washington Kastles Internship Program during the summer of 2015. You may contact me at (555) 555–5555 or student@umich.edu. Thank you for your time and consideration.

Sincerely,

Student's Signature

Student's Printed Name
Michigan Sport Management Program, Class of 2016

555 Acorn Dr., Ann Arbor, MI   student@umich.edu   555-555-5555

March 20, 2015

Fox Sports Detroit
26555 Evergreen Meadows Rd.
Southfield, MI 48076

Greetings Fox Sports Detroit Internship Coordinator:

I am interested in interning with Fox Sports Detroit in the summer of 2015. As a rising junior at the University of Michigan studying the business of sport, and a current staff writer for the Michigan Daily, I have developed strong written and oral communication skills, knowledge of the sport industry's business operations, and the ability to achieve goals independently and through collaborative efforts. I am confident I have the skills you desire in an intern at Fox Sports Detroit.

My coursework has provided me with extensive knowledge of the sport industry, including the communication, business, and societal factors that make sport such a unique commodity. My academic work is complemented by the skills I have gained as a staff writer for the Michigan Daily covering the Michigan men's soccer team. I cover weekly games and news regarding the team, and write and edit game stories for weekly publication. In addition, I contribute proposals in weekly staff meetings as we strategize the direction of Michigan's completely student-run publication that prints over 18,000 daily copies, five days per week. Based on the internship qualifications you have posted online, I am confident that my current studies and my work as a Michigan Daily sports writer make me a qualified candidate to work at a fast pace within time sensitive deadlines at Fox Sports Detroit.

I would appreciate the opportunity to discuss your summer internship opportunities. My winter semester at the University of Michigan concludes on April 29th and I am available to work as soon as May 1st. I am available via telephone at (555)555-5555 or email at student@umich.edu. Thank you for your consideration.

Sincerely,

Student's Signature

Student's Printed Name
Sport Management Program
University of Michigan
Class of 2016

In Summary:

1. Write a unique, one-page cover letter for each position to which you apply.

2. Follow formal writing rules, write concisely, organize clearly, and don't copy and paste the same language from your resume.

3. Address your cover letter to a specific person; make every effort to find the appropriate person's name.

4. Highlight your relevant experiences and skills in your cover letter by responding to those mentioned in the job posting.

5. Make an effort to gather more information on the position by talking to a current or former employee, or calling human resources.

6. Have your cover letter reviewed by multiple people before sending it out.

Chapter 4

Assembling Additional Application Materials

Chapter 4 Assembling Additional Application Materials

Most employers will require a resume and cover letter from internship applicants. Some employers may also ask for references, possibly recommendation letters, and even a copy of your academic transcript. As the internship applicant pool grows and the job market becomes more competitive, employers have also required personality tests, project-style assignments, or presentations to be completed as part of the application process.

While you may not be able to prepare all of these possible materials before starting your internship search, you should prepare those that you can. Your resume and cover letter, as well as your reference list and a portfolio of samples of your work, should be prepared in advance. This chapter will discuss your reference list and work portfolio.

Reference List

A reference list may include professional, academic, and/or personal references. Typically, employers will ask for two to three references and require that at least one of them be a former employer or someone who supervised you in a work environment. If you haven't held a paid position or an official internship, a supervisor may include a work study supervisor, or perhaps an instructor or academic advisor. As you prepare your reference list, you'll need to decide whom to ask to serve as a reference for you and you'll need to obtain each reference's approval to share her/his contact information with employers.

As you select your references, keep in mind that those who worked with you closely will be able to give potential employers the most detailed, and thus strongest, recommendation of your work. In other words, don't choose your references based on their job title. It's best to choose your direct supervisor who worked with you daily and was a "research assistant," rather than his boss who only saw you give one presentation, even if she was the "managing director." Employers will want to hear from those who worked with you closely and can describe your responsibilities, the tasks you completed, as well as your worth ethic, professionalism, and personality.

Again, you'll need each reference's consent to give her/his contact information to prospective employers. In addition, it's in your benefit to give your references advanced notice if you think an employer will be contacting them as this will allow your references to gather their thoughts and remind themselves of your specific work. It's also acceptable for you to politely request that your references share specific work you completed or specific qualities you consider relevant with potential employers.

You'll need to include each reference's name and title, employer, address, phone, and email on your reference list. The following example includes the same header used on the student's cover letter and resume.

STUDENT

| 55 Acorn Drive | Ann Arbor, MI 48109 | (555)-555-5555 | student@umich.edu |

Professional References
Jessica Lyndquist
Promotions Coordinator, Detroit Demolition
55 Radcliffe Lane, Detroit, MI 48243
(555)555-5555
lyndquist@detroitdemolition.com

Samuel Miazzo
Manager, Ernesto's Restaurant
55 Main Street, Ann Arbor, MI 48109
(555)555-5555
miazzo@ernestos.com

Academic Reference
Kelli Donahue
Associate Program Chair, Michigan Sport Management Program
University of Michigan
1402 Washington Heights, Ann Arbor, MI 48109
(555)555-5555
kjdonahu@umich.edu

As mentioned at the conclusion of the first chapter, for the purpose of printing your resume, cover letter, and reference list, it's worth the investment to buy some quality card stock. By the point of your sophomore year, you should be carrying numerous copies of your resume on you at all times. When snail mailing hard copies to employers, assemble your materials in the following order: 1) cover letter; 2) resume; and 3) your references and any additional materials.

When emailing an employer your application materials, attach your materials as PDFs rather than Word documents, as PDFs maintain their integrity no matter what software program a person is using. Name each document with your full name and the document title (e.g.: KelliDonahueCoverLetter, KelliDonahueResume, etc.).

Recommendation Letters

You may be required to include a recommendation letter for different types of applications, such as internships, study abroad programs, or graduate school programs. In each circumstance, you should choose whom to ask for a letter by considering what each possible source can say about you based on the context of your relationship and the work you have done for them. In most cases, your recommenders will write the letter for you; however, in some circumstances, recommenders have been known to ask you to write the letter yourself.

When requesting any type of recommendation letter, the following rules apply:

- Allow your recommender at least two to three weeks to write the letter.

- Include all necessary details in your request: the date by which you need the letter; the specific person or organization to whom the letter should be addressed; whether the letter be electronic or hard copy and the corresponding link or mailing address (if a mailing address, it is also courteous to include a stamped and addressed envelope).

- Attach your most recent resume to your emailed request; also attach any other materials that may assist your recommender in personalizing your letter, such as your statement of purpose, academic transcript, the job posting, etc. It is acceptable to request that your recommender mention specific traits, qualities, or work you have done for them.

- If a semester or more has passed since you last interacted with your recommender, remind them of which course you took with them and the semester in which you took it, or when and in what role you worked for them.

- Send a thank you note via email or snail mail (or both) after the letter has been completed/submitted. Gifts are also welcome ☺

If a potential employer requires a recommendation letter, it's generally most beneficial for you to ask a former employer to write the letter. If you don't have a former employer to ask, you may request a letter from an academic source. In this case, it's best if the academic recommender has known you for at least one full semester or more. If you intend to apply to graduate school, you'll need a recommendation letter from an academic source, or in some cases, two to three letters. An academic source includes faculty, research staff, graduate student instructors, or your academic advisor.

Letters from Employers

Most people you ask will only agree to write you a recommendation letter if they're confident they can write you a positive letter. This requires that the recommender know you, your qualities, and the work you have completed well; therefore, it's best to request a letter while you're fresh in their minds. Even if you don't expect that you'll need a recommendation letter in the immediate future, it's best to request one from an internship employer right before your internship employment ends; for example, if you excelled in your internship with IMG and would like to request a recommendation letter from your supervisor to have in your files, you should request a recommendation letter about two weeks before your internship concludes.

When you request a recommendation letter, also send your supervisor a brief summary of the tasks/projects you completed as an intern. An electronic copy is best so that she/he can reference it. This will give your employer specific points to include in your letter.

Consider the same advice we discussed in seeking out references. Those who know you best and worked with you most directly will write more specific, and thus stronger, recommendation letters.

The completed letter should be written on the organization's letterhead and include your employer's signature. Ask for an electronic copy as a PDF (or scan it/convert it yourself), so you'll have it anytime you need it in the future. It's also acceptable (and a good idea) to give your employer a specific date by which you would like to receive the letter. It'll be easier to follow up on the letter before you leave the office rather than via email or phone, which is why you should request the letter about two weeks prior to the conclusion of your internship.

Letters from Academic Sources

If you're in need of an academic source to write a recommendation letter, you'll want to choose someone who has gotten to know you on a more personally professional level. This means you should have attended office hours, spoken with your faculty and staff before and/or after class, attended class consistently and participated in course discussions. Do not ask for a recommendation letter from an academic source unless you have known that person for at least a full semester.

If you're requesting a letter in advance of when you'll need it, you can make use of the University of Michigan's Career Center Reference Letter Service. The Career Center will keep your letters on file for you (for a small fee) and will send them out as you need them. For further details, please go to the Career Center's Reference Letter Service site: http://www.careercenter.umich.edu/content/reference-letter-service

The Career Center will only accept general letters, which means a letter that is not addressed to a specific employer/organization/school and which does not reference a specific position. While this will work in most cases, when possible, a letter that directly addresses the graduate school or internship/permanent position to which you are applying will be stronger than a general letter.

Writing Your Own Recommendation Letter
In many cases, employers, particularly summer internship employers, will ask you to write your own recommendation letter. As long as your

employer *reads the final letter and signs her/his signature,* she/he is endorsing you as a potential candidate and this is fine.

Writing your own recommendation letter may seem like a daunting task, but it can also be a really good thing. You can cater the letter to include specifics that will be most valuable in your future job searches.

As you prepare your recommendation letter, keep in mind that a recommendation letter is typically one page and follows a standard business letter format with three to four paragraphs. Strong recommendation letters mention specific things that you worked on, specific responsibilities and/or tasks you completed.

The first paragraph of a recommendation letter should indicate the purpose of the letter (to recommend you) and should give the context in which the recommender has known you. The first paragraph may also include a preview sentence that mentions your specific skills/accomplishments, for example:

> I strongly recommend Calvin Brady for a position with your organization. Calvin worked as an intern with the Leverage Agency this past summer. As his direct supervisor, I trusted Calvin with significant responsibility. I have been pleased with his work and he has been a valuable addition to our staff.

The second and possible third paragraphs should describe the specific tasks/responsibilities of your internship and the positive results of your work. A second paragraph could include:

> Calvin has strong communication skills. He contacted our clients daily via phone and email to schedule meetings. He also attended meetings with our marketing and promotions department on my behalf. On two separate occasions, I was unable to attend meetings and asked Calvin to deliver brief presentations in my absence. In the first presentation he summarized our most recent target sales projections and in the second he presented my recommendations for changes to a major client proposal. I received positive feedback on his presentations and was told that he demonstrated professional presentation skills and spoke with confidence and clarity.

The final paragraph should close the letter, provide one final statement confidently recommending the applicant, and include the recommender's contact information:

> Once again, I confidently recommend Calvin Brady for a position with your organization. He is a competent employee who will exceed your expectations. You may reach me at (555)555-5555 or (employer@email.com) if you would like further information.

Remember, in the case of having to write your own recommendation letter, the final letter should be on official organization letterhead, should be read by the recommender, signed, and given to you as an electronic copy for you to keep on file. As for all recommendations, send a thank you note upon receiving the final, signed letter.

Send a Thank You Note

Once you receive a final recommendation letter, or it has been submitted, or one of your references has been contacted via phone/email to provide a recommendation for you, you should send a thank you note. You may thank your recommender in person (small tokens of appreciation, such as chocolate, are also thoughtful), though you should still send an emailed or snail-mailed (or both) thank you note. I highly recommend a hand-written card if you want to make a lasting impression.

Curriculum Vitae

In addition to the previously discussed application materials, employers may request additional documents. Even if not requested, it can be to your benefit to prepare and include additional documents in your application, like a curriculum vitae or a portfolio of your work. E-portfolios will be discussed further in Chapter 5 Promoting Your Brand and Building Your Network.

A curriculum vitae (CV) can be a beneficial additional document to include in your application materials. It's similar to a business resume in that its purpose is to highlight your skills and experiences; however, a CV goes beyond your business experiences and includes relevant academic experiences as well. For this reason, it can be beneficial to include if you'd like to show the employer relevant classes or class projects. Typically, the most relevant coursework/projects that make sense to highlight on a CV are completed in your upper-level coursework during your junior and senior year. A CV is not recommended for freshmen or sophomore-level students.

A CV is organized similarly to a resume with the use of headers and bulleted descriptions. It should follow reverse chronological order while listing bullets in decreasing order of importance. The same rules apply for formatting and wording that were discussed in the resume section. Unlike your resume, which should be one page at this time, your CV may extend to two pages.

When writing your bulleted descriptions for course projects, describe the purpose of the project, the process of completion, and the end result. You should also include if it was a collaborative effort or individually completed. In the case of collaborative work, be sure to indicate your individual responsibilities and contributions.

A CV should be included as a complement to your resume, not in place of the resume. Your CV name/address header should match that of your resume. The following pages include a sample two-page CV.

YOUR NAME

student@umich.edu   555-555-5555   43 Acorn Rd, Ann Arbor, MI 48109

EDUCATION
University of Michigan, Ann Arbor, MI
Bachelor of Arts Degree in Sport Management, Expected May 2014

RELEVANT COURESWORK

Brand Strategy & Advertising Campaigns	Sport Finance
Principles of Marketing	Legal Issues in Sport & Fitness
Sponsorship Linked Marketing	Sales Management
Economics of Sport	Business Communications
Sports, Economic Development & Urban Revitalization	

ACADEMIC PROJECTS

Sponsorship Linked Marketing   Winter 2014
- Collaborated with group members to create and pitch a sponsorship partnership between the Detroit Tigers and Chobani Yogurt
- Researched Tigers' fans demographics and Tigers' current sponsors to prepare targeted campaign for Chobani; interviewed Tigers' Vice President of Corporate Sponsorships Steve Harms and Chobani Vice President of Marketing Doren Stern; conducted survey of over 200 Tigers' fans via email to 2013 season-ticket holders
- Individually created visual of proposed Chobani marketing displays and booths to be erected in Comerica Park concourse; created visuals in Adobe Photoshop and InDesign; prepared large poster sample for presentation
- Presented final proposal with group members to Steve Harms and Professor Dae Hee Kwak of Michigan Sport Management Program; received positive feedback from Tigers' executive and a final grade of A for the project

Sales Management   Fall 2013
- Developed knowledge and ability to execute sales calls and adjust pitches based on target consumers' needs
- Demonstrated ability to sell diverse products and services through in-class presentations and role plays; polished communication skills via phone, business email, and in-person conversations
- Collaborated with group members to prepare a sales pitch to the University of Michigan Hockey team from Locker Room to sell an iPad app; final sales call video is viewable via You Tube at www.youtube.555555

ORGANIZATIONS & MEMBERSHIPS

VP of Marketing, Michigan Club Sports   September 2013 – April 2014
- Created and distributed marketing flyers, brochures, & email blasts to market club sports to students to increase participation in 30+ sports
- Designed promotional t-shirt; researched vendors and finalized order of over 500 t-shirts for promotional giveaway at Fall Festival
- Increased membership in 2013-2014 academic year by over 5% from previous year; increase largely attributed to successful, continuous marketing

Member, Sport Business Association   September 2011 – April 2014
- Developed knowledge of sport industry by attending membership meetings, guest presentations, and on-site visits with leading sport organizations, such as the Detroit Pistons and the New York Mets
- Participated in networking events; developed excellent communication skills and the ability to converse with diverse others in a professional setting

In Summary:

1. Prepare a reference list to include in your application materials.
   a. Ask your recommenders for permission to include their contact information. Two to three recommenders are fairly standard: three professional, or two professional and one academic.
   b. Give recommenders advanced notice if you know they'll be contacted by an employer.
   c. Request that your recommenders share specific traits, skills, or experiences with employers to best sell you.
2. Be prepared to ask for recommendation letters, and possibly write your own.
   a. When letters are required, provide your recommenders with at least two weeks notice and all necessary details to write the letter, including submission information.
   b. Request a recommendation letter from your internship supervisor two weeks prior to the end of your internship.
   c. If your supervisor asks you to write it yourself, follow the guidelines in this chapter and have your supervisor read and sign the final letter.
   d. Completed letters should be on organization letterhead, signed, and sent to you as PDFs.
3. Send all recommenders thank you notes within a week of their recommendation. Hand written cards are preferred and small tokens of appreciation make a lasting impression.
4. Consider preparing a CV to complement your application materials and include it in addition to (not in place of) your business resume.

Chapter 5

Building Your Network & Promoting Your Brand

Chapter 5 Building Your Network & Promoting Your Brand

According to the U.S. Bureau of Labor Statistics, 70% of all jobs are found through networking. Some college recruiters have posted that number as being upwards of 80%. In the sport industry, most industry professionals will tell you that the number is really closer to 90%.

These statistics may seem daunting, but while networking may be time consuming, it's actually a fairly painless process. With the use of email, LinkedIn, social media, numerous guest speaker events on campus, and Michigan's own Sport Business Conference (MSBC), your immediate opportunities to network are vast. The key is to start your networking early (now if you haven't started already) and to record your networking connections. This can be done via LinkedIn and, as discussed earlier, I also suggest creating a master database to keep track of your contacts' information and details of their internship application processes. You should be adding new connections to this database each semester and checking in with connections you have made periodically throughout your time at Michigan.

Our Sport Management students who have taken the time to build such databases and foster relationships with their connections have secured employment upon graduation faster than their peers who did not have extensive networks. This is because the sport industry, though worth approximately $485 billion in the US market alone according to Plunkett Research, Ltd. (2014), is actually quite small and well networked. Many internship opportunities and full-time positions are never posted to on-line recruiting sites as employers have found greater success in hiring and promoting from internal candidates or from referrals and recommendations received from others in their network. Such referrals allow employers to get a sense of a candidate's job performance and work ethic through the observations of others they trust and respect.

Partially due to the fact that the sport industry is small and well networked, and also because of the nature of the business, employers look for industry-specific experience when hiring full-time employees. In other words, you must obtain relevant, sport-industry experience prior to graduation to have any realistic hope of working in the sport industry after graduation. This is all great news for students who have had the opportunity to intern at various organizations, establish themselves as excellent employees, and build their professional networks. However, for those of you who have not yet held an internship in the sport industry, the importance of obtaining your first internship adds a sense of urgency to the process.

This chapter will focus first on establishing your personal, professional brand so that you are putting forth a professional, goal-oriented, competent image of yourself to employers. We'll also discuss promoting your brand and networking to build your professional connections.

Establishing Your Personal, Professional Brand

Your personal, professional brand should be reflected in your image online and in person, as well as in all of your correspondence with employers, your LinkedIn profile and all other social media activity, business cards, and application materials (e.g.: resume, cover letter, portfolio materials, etc.).

The following general rules should be considered as you establish your brand:

Choose one name to use on all of your documents and communications with employers. This may be your full first name and last name; or your nickname and last name; or your full first name, full middle name, and last name; or perhaps your full first name, middle initial, and last name. My personal preference is to use your full first name rather than a nickname because it generally looks more formal and professional and there's something substantial about a name that takes up more space in the header of your resume and on your business card. This doesn't mean that you have to go by your full first name once hired. If your name is Catherine and you go by Cate, you can ask your employer and colleagues to call you Cate once you're hired or even later in the interviewing process.

Use one phone number and your Michigan email. As you begin to connect with employers and share your contact information, choose which phone number and email you'll use. Most likely, you'll be using your cell number, in which case, be sure your outgoing message is appropriately professional. Once you begin applying for positions or seeking out opportunities to connect with employers via informational interviews, don't answer a phone call if it is unexpected and you're not in a quiet place. Instead, let the call go to voice mail, check the message immediately, and move to a quiet place so that you may call the employer and have a professional conversation. This also allows you a few moments to mentally focus. If you should receive the employer's voicemail, leave a message with some additional times in which you will be available for her/him to call you back (within business hours) and be sure that you're ready to receive a call during one of the times given so you don't miss the employer's call a second time.

It's recommended that you use your Michigan email rather than another account simply to capitalize on the power of the Michigan brand.

Set Up Your Email Signature. If you haven't already done so, set up your email signature. The directions to do so can easily be found in the mail help menu. Your signature should include your full name. This allows you to end your email message by typing a closing (e.g.: "Sincerely," "Best," "Warm Regards," etc.) and your first name only, which personalizes the email message. Beneath this closing, your signature should include your full name, your program/major and graduation year, and any leadership positions you may hold in campus organizations. You may also choose to include your email address in case your email message is printed and possibly your cell phone number. Your signature should be between two lines (including your name) and five or six lines. An example was provided in our section on cover letters. Here is another:

> Brett Wolverine
> Treasurer, Sport Business Association
> Michigan Sport Management Program, Class of 2015
> University of Michigan
> bthestudent@umich.edu   (555-555)-5555

Choose a font and colors strategically and use them consistently. Carefully select the font style and color(s) you use for your name on your resume, business cards, email tag line, printed portfolio materials, e-portfolio, and anywhere else your name appears. Your materials look very polished and professional when you have consistency in the font style and colors used on these materials. Also, as you foster a relationship with professionals, it will help them remember you if your various forms of communication and documents appear with consistency over time. Remember, the general rule of graphic design is to use no more than two font styles on each document (you may use three on the resume if one is used for your name and two others are used consistently for all other text: one for headers and one for descriptive text).

Font styles elicit different meanings or feelings. Comic sans, for example, is informal and not recommended for professional documents while Times New Roman is fairly standard and professional (but also a tad boring). Spend some time checking out different font styles and find one that appears professional, easy to read, and fits your personality. Stay away from those that are script-style as they can be difficult to read.

You want your name to pop and be read quickly, so have it appear in a larger size font, and possibly in bold, when appropriate and space allows. The name in the sample email signature line earlier (Brett Wolverine) is in the font style of Georgia and is one and a half sizes larger than the font in the rest of the signature line. Ideally, this same font style would be used for Brett's name on his resume, cover letter, electronic portfolio, etc.

Colors, like font styles, also elicit different feelings. Strong, bold colors come across as more powerful than pastel colors and are also easier to read in print. Color use on the resume is not standard, though a limited use of coordinating, easy-to read-color for the header, or possibly the header and organization names, can appear professional and make your resume stand out. This can be useful for marketing or event planning positions when creativity is encouraged. For business operations or financial positions within the industry, black resume text is recommended.

The Michigan Alumni Association will print about 30 business cards for current students for free (check out their website for dates). If you have your business cards printed through the Alumni Association, they'll come with the Michigan maize and blue color branding and a block 'M'. You can carry this color branding to your e-portfolio by using maize and blue as a complementary color (not your main text color, maize isn't easy to read). We'll discuss color and font use for the e-portfolio much more in class as we near this assignment.

Order Business Cards. As you begin attending guest speaker, career fair, networking, and conference events, you'll want to have a number of business cards readily available to exchange with industry professionals. You may also choose to clip a business card to the top of your resume when handing or mailing someone a hard copy. Your business card is an extension of your personal, professional brand. Consider our discussion of font style and color use, and carefully consider what to include on your business card. At a minimum, you will include your full name (the name you have chosen to use in your branding), major, U-M, and graduation year. It's also recommended that you include your personalized LinkedIn URL and your e-portfolio URL. You may also include a leadership position as you may have done in your email signature line, and even a catchy tag line similar to that in your LinkedIn headline (more on that in the next section).

As mentioned, the Michigan Alumni Association offers to print every Michigan student 30 free business cards (They also offer free blue books in their office at 200 Fletcher Street). Details can be found on-line via the Alumni Association website at:

http://alumni.umich.edu/students/business-cards-blue-books

If you wish to order additional business cards, there are a number of retailers that offer affordable prices, such as Vista Print (vistaprint.com).

Take advantage of the power of the Michigan name. The block 'M' is a widely recognized university logo, rated in 2012 by Bleacher Report as the second most-widely-recognized college football logo in the world (second only to Notre Dame). While the university has strict restrictions on using the Block M, you can use the University of Michigan name and perhaps subtle use or Maize and Blue (recommended as complementary color, not for font colors as they can be hard to read).

It's also recommended that you use "Michigan Sport Management Program" as the title of your home program. For the purpose of your application materials and branding, drop "School of Kinesiology" as the Sport Management Program's name will carry the most recognition in the industry. Remember, consistency is key, so whatever you choose to use, use the same language on all of your documents and communications.

Using LinkedIn & Other Social Media Accounts

According to LinkedIn's published statistics, the site reached 300 million users in April of 2014 with 100 million of these users in the US. LinkedIn consultant Wayne Breitbarth reported in Forbes in 2014 that over 50% of users have over 500 connections and that 48% of survey responders indicated using the site for two or more hours per week. The site is growing in users and in user usage. As a business tool it has proven very effective for professionals making connections, job hunters seeking opportunities, and employers seeking qualified applicants. A number of job seekers have reported going to interviews where employers have printed out their LinkedIn profiles in lieu of their resumes.

Create Your LinkedIn Account & Build Your Profile

If you're new to LinkedIn, you'll need to begin by creating an account at linkedin.com. LinkedIn will prompt you to provide information as you get started. You'll be asked to build your profile, upload a picture, and create a headline. Remember, your LinkedIn account is part of your branding, your online image. You'll want to spend time developing your profile to promote your professional image, and then continue to update your account often to remain current and to continue to appear in your contacts' feeds.

When potential contacts search for you on LinkedIn, your picture and headline appear in search results. This means your picture and headline are of the utmost importance as they establish your first impression and compel employers to connect with you so that they may view your entire profile. Your picture should be professional in its quality and in your appearance; business professional attire is ideal. On occasion throughout the academic year, the Kinesiology OUSA, SBA, or MSBC may make professional photographers available for you to have a high-quality headshot taken. When planning your professional attire for your headshot, follow the same guidelines as you would for an interview. Interview attire is discussed in Chapter 6.

Your LinkedIn headline is like your tag line, a quick snapshot of you, perhaps your goals, and your skills and/or experience. As an example, let's assume you're currently involved in an internship search and your goal is to work with a professional sports team in community relations. Your headline might be: "Michigan Sport Management student seeking internship in community relations with professional sports team." This headline lets employers know you're available and actively seeking an internship. If you're not actively engaged in an internship search, or you're currently interning with an organization, a more general headline indicating your current position would be appropriate: "Michigan student studying the business of sport/Current IMG Properties Assistant."

Next, you'll need to build your LinkedIn profile by responding to LinkedIn's prompts. Your profile should be approached similarly to your resume in that your purpose is to inform viewers of your education, experiences, and skills; however, you don't want to simply copy and paste your resume. Use your profile to tell more of your story, and expand on your past experiences in more detail than your resume allows. You may attach your actual resume to your profile as a PDF.

Many recruiters have expressed a preference for creative profiles, profiles that read with more personal voice. In fact, your profile may read more like a *brief* essay of your professional experiences – "brief" being the key word. Like your resume, employers will spend little time reading your profile, so you want to organize your information in decreasing order of importance and make use of formatting (e.g.: bold, italics, white space, larger font sizes, etc.) to make your key information pop.

Once you have completed your profile, read LinkedIn's information on managing your profile, filing and organizing your contacts, etc. It's also very helpful to attend a LinkedIn workshop to learn more and watch tutorials on using the site most effectively. The Michigan Alumni Association and the Michigan Career Center provide workshops and on-line tutorials at various times throughout the year. Check their websites for more information.

As you build and manage your LinkedIn presence to promote your professional brand, it's helpful to browse other students' and industry professionals' LinkedIn headlines and profiles for examples. As with your resume and cover letter, you should also seek feedback on your profile from trusted advisors, including professionals in the field you intend to work.

Make Connections & Build Professional Relationships
As you're building your LinkedIn network, your goal is to increase your number of connections and establish professional relationships with relevant contacts. Eventually, after you communicate with a connection through LinkedIn messages, email exchanges, and/or informational interviews via phone, you may want ask a connection to review your profile or resume and give you feedback. This is not something you immediately ask of a new connection. You only do so after developing your professional relationship.

Once you connect with someone on LinkedIn, they're considered a first-degree contact. Your first-degree contacts' contacts are second-degree contacts to you, and your second-degree contacts' contacts are third-degree contacts to you. When you conduct a search on LinkedIn, you'll only see results for people who are connected to your network up to a third-degree contact. So, the more first-degree connections you have the larger your entire network.

Start building your network by connecting with your Michigan peers, faculty, and staff first, as well as any former employers or family on LinkedIn. Then, work on building your network of relevant industry professionals by tapping into the Michigan alumni network. Use the LinkedIn search box to search for alumni who work for organizations or in positions in which you're interested. Include "University of Michigan" and the organization name as key words; for example, you might search for "University of Michigan and IMG." Alternatively, if you have a position or job title in mind but not a specific organization, you can search with that information; for example, you might search for "University of Michigan and director of media relations."

Once you find an alum with whom you're interested in connecting, familiarize yourself with her/his background. Read as much as you can about them on LinkedIn and do a Google search to find other sources of information. Then, use this information to send each person with whom you wish to connect a personalized message. *Do not request to connect with someone without a personalized message.* In your message you should introduce yourself and include your status as a current Michigan Sport Management student. Then, indicate your interest in connecting; for example:

> *Greetings Mr. Brown:*
>
> *My name is Jessica Observatory and I am currently a sophomore at the University of Michigan in the Sport Management Program. This past summer I interned with Fox Sports Detroit as a media intern. I am interested in pursuing a career in media, perhaps as a sports analyst and would like to learn more about your path to success.*
>
> *Thank you for your time and I look forward to connecting with you.*
> *Sincerely,*
> *Jessica*
>
> *Jessica Observatory*
> *Sport Management Class of 2017*
> *University of Michigan*
> *student@umich.edu   (555)-555-5555*

If this connection is accepted, your next message should request an informational phone interview or email exchange so that you may learn more about Mr. Brown and establish a professional relationship with him. Don't ask him to review your resume or help you find an internship. Again, you need to build the relationship first before making a request. To do so earlier is considered very bad form.

In addition to searching for Sport Management alumni and University of Michigan alumni from other majors, you should also be attending guest speaker events, networking events, career fairs, and any other opportunities to interact and network with industry professionals. After each of these events, search for the industry professional via LinkedIn and send them a connection request. Your personalized message should follow the advice given earlier by beginning with an introduction. Then, indicate the event at which you recently met or at which you heard this person speak. If you were able to speak with them, mention something specific that the two of you spoke about. Even if they don't remember you, this will be appreciated and increase the likelihood that they'll accept your connection request.

As a side note, if you're able to spend time speaking with someone at an event, take the opportunity to ask for a business card. Then, send your message directly to their business email as this is often even more effective in getting a response than a LinkedIn message.

Be Active and Use Linked In to Promote Your Professional Brand
As you're making connections and gathering contact information on industry professionals, you should be adding this information to your master employer database. Maintain a list in your database of "special contacts," professionals with whom you would like to foster a closer

professional relationship because they either work for or are in close contact with organizations you have an interest in working. Then, focus on staying actively engaged with these professionals via LinkedIn. You can do so by conducting an informational interview as discussed, and then continuing to send messages every eight to twelve weeks. This is sufficient to keep the relationship growing. Your message might include an update on your recent professional or educational experiences, or a quick discussion of recent, relevant industry news.

In addition to maintaining contact with individuals in your network, you can be active on LinkedIn by joining relevant groups (LinkedIn allows you to follow up to 50 groups) and engaging in these groups' discussions. You can also follow relevant organizations. In addition, you can continue to pop into people's LinkedIn news feeds by posting status updates. These updates could announce your recent accomplishments, comment on relevant current events, or post links to relevant news stories. Remember, everything you post is tied to your on-line image, so post information that promotes the image you want employers to see. The more active you are on LinkedIn the more you will appear in your connections' LinkedIn updates and feeds.

Not every connection you make on LinkedIn will prove helpful to you in your job or internship search, but remember, the more relevant first-degree connections you have the stronger your overall network.

Make the Most of Your Other Social Media Accounts
Once you begin actively promoting your professional brand, you should be monitoring your entire on-line presence. This includes LinkedIn and any other social media accounts you use, such as Facebook, Twitter, Instagram, etc.

It goes without saying that you should keep a "clean" presence on-line. If you don't already have the highest security on your social apps, adjust your security settings now and do your best to ensure any photographs or postings in which your image or name are mentioned are appropriate. Also, remember that as a Michigan Sport Management student, you now represent yourself, the Michigan Sport Management Program, and the University of Michigan. This should not be taken lightly. You have a reputation of excellence to uphold.

Some students have asked if it's safer to drop out of social media entirely. This is not recommended. Employers typically search for candidates on-line as part of their review process and your absence from social media may actually raise a red flag.

Your social media accounts may be used somewhat differently, but all should be used to project the image you want to promote. Facebook has fairly good security if applied correctly, and may be used as more of your "friend and family app" to post more personal information. Instagram and Twitter should be used more strategically to promote your professional image. Twitter, particularly, should be thought of as "Main Street," a place where all can access your posts. Use this to your benefit by following relevant people/organizations and posting relevant updates like educational/internship status updates, comments on recent news, or links to relevant stories.

Many of our recent Sport Management students have worked in social media positions for various organizations where they have conducted research or run the organization's social media accounts. In such cases, employers will absolutely analyze your social media presence as part of their candidate review process. At a minimum, employers will look to ensure you keep a respectful on-line social presence, one that will not embarrass the organization. In the event that social media is part of the position to which you are applying, the employer will look more closely to see if you are engaged on social media in a way that is relevant to the industry.

Think carefully before posting and don't underestimate the power of a tweet. One of our 2015 alum, Shannon Lynch, had a tweet about the *Saturday Night Live* 40th Anniversary show retweeted by *Saturday Night Live.* For a student aspiring to work in social media for a professional sports team, this provided an excellent (and very memorable) story to share in interviews.

Creating an E-Portfolio

As your final project in this course, you'll create and publish an e-portfolio. We'll discuss your e-portfolio extensively in class and we'll look at sample e-portfolios of former students. Your e-portfolio should promote your personal, professional brand. You should carefully consider the font style, text size, color and images that you use so that your portfolio best promotes the image you want employers to see of you.

The e-portfolio promotes your professional brand through its appearance, as well as the content you post. It should include a brief professional biography, similar to your LinkedIn profile and resume. You'll post samples of your written work like news releases, sales pitches, etc. You'll also include samples of your design work, like PowerPoint or Prezi presentations, logo designs you've created, links to external website design, etc. You're required to post a number of assignments from this class to your portfolio for your final project. These details are found on your e-portfolio assignment sheet.

Going forward, it's my hope that you'll include your portfolio URL on your business card, as well as on your resume, LinkedIn account and in your email signature. Ideally, you continue to revise and add to your portfolio as you progress in your education and your professional experiences after this class. The e-portfolio has proven to be an effective tool in students' job searches for those who have continued to revise and update the portfolio during their junior and senior years.

One of the best examples of this is Nicole Anderson, SM Class of 2011. During her final interview for a post-graduate internship at Nike, the interviewers (there were two on the phone) were browsing her portfolio. They spent a few minutes asking Nicole questions about her work; she had included many writing and design projects from upper-level SM coursework and from previous internships. After the interview, they told Nicole they were impressed with her work and that she had taken the time to create a portfolio. It had distinguished her from other applicants.

The results were successful as Nicole was given, and accepted, a post-graduate internship offer. I'm sure the offer was extended based on more than the e-portfolio. Nicole's work samples were excellent, her communication skills strong, and she was well prepared for the interviewers' questions. Based on the interviewers' feedback, however, the e-portfolio was well received and made a positive impact.

Even more recently, Ally Futterman, who took SM 217 during the winter of 2014, was interviewing with the NY Mets for a summer 2014 internship. After she received the internship and had been working for a week or two, her boss told her that her e-portfolio was a major reason they extended her a job offer as they thought it showed great professional initiative and they were impressed with the work samples she had included.

Again, we'll discuss your e-portfolio assignment in class as the end of the semester nears. In the meantime, you can read the assignment sheet to get a feel for what the e-portfolio will include, or to start working on your portfolio early.

Crafting Your Elevator Pitch

When you attend a networking event or find yourself in a position to introduce yourself to someone with whom you'd like to connect, you have very little time to make a positive, and lasting, first impression.

Your introduction in such situations is referred to as your "elevator pitch."

An elevator pitch should be carefully crafted to promote your brand. It's a constant evolution that changes as your experiences evolve at Michigan and in your professional endeavors.

Your elevator pitch should quickly establish your credibility, your career interests, and include something unique so that the person with whom your speaking will remember you when you send an email or LinkedIn request to connect. If you find yourself with more than a handful of minutes to engage in conversation with a prospective connection, you'll want to have done your research ahead of time so you can drive the conversation by asking questions about the person's background, her/his organization, or recent industry news.

Your introduction of yourself should begin with your full name and your initiation of a firm handshake accompanied by strong eye contact. Then, include a little of your background information. Your elevator pitch may adjust slightly as you meet different people to strategically include information that would most effectively appeal to each person's career areas. As an example, hypothetically assume you find yourself in a position to meet U-M Assistant Athletic Media Relations Director Leah Howard. You've thought about pursuing media relations as a career path and you have a special interest in softball, one of the sports that Leah manages.

Your previous internship/work experience includes two positions from the previous summer: 1) you worked as a program intern for your high school athletic department coordinating fall team schedules, writing and printing game programs, and updating team websites; and 2) you worked as a softball coach for your former high school team.

You want to make a favorable impression on Leah (who you will address as "Ms. Howard" until invited to be on a first name basis), so you can develop a professional relationship and reach out in the future for advice or possible internship opportunities. Begin by extending your hand for a handshake and introducing yourself with your full name, your status as a current Sport Management student, and a brief description of your two experiences from the previous summer. In this situation, both of your previous experiences are relevant as they demonstrate strong organization skills and writing skills, as well as knowledge of softball. Include a brief description of your internship duties in your introduction and mention that these experiences helped shape your career aspirations to work for an athletic department.

From there, provided you have time, you can continue the conversation with Ms. Howard by asking about her background. Ideally, you did some research ahead of time so that you're aware that she graduated from Michigan with a B.A. in Economics and Communications and an M.A. in Sport Management. It's likely the two of you have shared faculty and staff. Knowing this, you could ask Leah, *"Which of your graduate classes did you find the most interesting or relevant to what you are doing now?"* or *"Are there any SM faculty you would suggest I get to know better or reach out to for professional advice?"* or *"Did you complete any internships in the area that you think would be beneficial for me to pursue given that I'd like to work in athletics?"*

These questions are somewhat open ended so Ms. Howard would end up doing most of the talking (which is wonderful, especially if you're still feeling nervous about talking yourself). They show you've done your research and you're interested in her and her accomplishments. They also give you memorable material to reference when you reach out to Ms. Howard later through email or LinkedIn.

Remember, you should adjust your elevator pitch strategically to best appeal to each person you meet and for each position for which you interview. An elevator pitch is the beginning of the "sell" process in any interview, even if it occurs for the first time at a career fair long before the interview takes place. Practice your elevator pitch many times and seek feedback from your trusted advisors. It's a constant work in progress and should evolve as your experiences progress.

In Summary:

1. Promote your professional brand by maintaining consistency in your materials. Use the same form of your name on your resume, cover letter, email signature, business cards, LinkedIn profile, e-portfolio, etc. You can further your brand by using the same font style and color scheme when appropriate as well.

2. Create your LinkedIn profile and build your network by requesting connections with Michigan alum and industry professionals; always send a personal message when requesting a connection.

3. Develop professional relationships with your connections by requesting informational interviews and continuing to send email updates about once every 8 to 12 weeks. Don't request help with your job search (e.g.: resume/cover letter reviews, assistance making another connection, etc.) until you've established a professional relationship.

4. Stay active on LinkedIn by posting status updates and links to relevant industry news.

5. Monitor all of your social media use to promote your professional brand and demonstrate knowledge and interest in your intended field.

6. Create an e-portfolio to differentiate yourself from other candidates in the job market. Include samples of your written and design work, as well as overviews of previous internship and/or relevant work experience.

7. Carefully craft your elevator pitch to quickly establish credibility and make a connection with each new contact or employer. Continuously revise your elevator pitch as you gain new experiences and skills. Seek feedback from trusted advisors.

Chapter 6

Interviewing *Successfully*

Chapter 6 Interviewing *Successfully*

As mentioned earlier, one of the hardest parts of the job search is simply getting chosen for an interview. Once you've scheduled an interview, you're in excellent position. Employers won't waste their time interviewing a candidate they don't believe to be qualified. The interview is your opportunity to confirm this and sell yourself as the most qualified and competent candidate for the job, which requires showing more than competence – you must also be likable.

This chapter will help you interview successfully by providing tips on interview preparation, execution, and follow up.

Interview Preparation

Before applying for a position, you should have conducted research on the organization and the position to cater your resume and cover letter to fit the position's responsibilities. Ideally, you've recorded helpful information in your master spreadsheet. Once you're asked for an interview, it's time to review this information and expand on your initial research.

Preparing for an interview should be approached with as much time and effort, possibly even more so, than you would dedicate to an academic course project. This cannot be stressed enough. Too many students have reported that they knew the exact moment when they failed an interview. More often than not that moment occurred because they were unable to answer specific questions about the company and the position for which they had applied. These questions have been things as simple as: *What intrigues you most about this position? What can you tell me about this job?* To things as complicated as: *Which one of our most recent commercials do you think was the most successful and why? Which one of our promotional events did you think was most effective last season?*

Before you start stressing out about these more challenging questions, let's start with the easier ones.

Employers will typically start an interview by asking you questions about yourself to get to know you and your qualifications further. As the interview progresses, they'll usually ask you specific questions about the job or area of the company in which you would work, as well as questions about the organization's recent business. They may even ask you to discuss recent business news affecting their competition. You should prepare responses for these types of questions by conducting thorough research of the organization and the industry. You can also attempt an informational interview with a previous intern, or a previous or current employee.

The more you know about the organization and the position the better you can prepare your application materials and your interview responses. Just as your cover letter varies for each position to which you apply, your interview responses may need to vary for each position for which you interview. By knowing what the position's responsibilities entail, you can best cater your answers to include the specific skills that are necessary to succeed in the job.

As you prepare for a successful interview, your research may include the following sources:

- The company's website and published literature
- Business and financial magazines, newspapers, and postings
- Your professional and personal network
- LinkedIn/Twitter/Facebook - find Michigan alumni, current students, or others who have previously worked for this company
- Call into the company's human resource department and ask to conduct a brief informational interview with one of their employees

General information to research on each organization should include:

- Position responsibilities: know the daily tasks and responsibilities for the position to which you applied, major assignments, to whom the position reports, whether the work will mainly be completed individually or as a group (expect a lot of group work for the majority of sport internships)

- Size of organization; domestic and international locations

- Organizational chart: know the divisions/departments, what each does, which location(s) they function out of, who is in charge of each, and approximately how many employees work in each

- Organizational culture: be familiar with office attire, office culture, approximate work load for employees, etc.

- If the organization is a team or league, be familiar with the rules of the game, recent transactions, stadium details, ticket plans, promotional packages, partnerships, fan attendance, league developments, TV and media contracts, etc.

- Competition: know who the organization's main competitors are and be familiar with their recent operations

- Financial situation: research the organization's financial situation; be familiar with top-selling products, poor-selling products, target consumer, etc.

As Sport Management students, many of you will apply for internships with sports teams or leagues. In this situation, especially if it's a sports team, you must be knowledgeable about the organization's business operations, such as their recent promotional events, stadium construction, changes in ticket packages, sponsorship of the organization, community relations/events, etc. You'll also want to know about recent trades, team performance, individual players, etc.

It's especially important in these situations to remember that you must appear as a competent professional, not merely another fan. There's a definite line between the two. The NFL isn't going to hire you if you don't know how many players take the field for a game – this exact question was asked by an NFL employee as one of my students was interviewing with them a few years ago. In the same interview, this student was also asked to name five of the team's sponsors and explain which relationship he thought was the most important for the team's success. He wasn't able to answer either question, an issue of nerves and poor preparation. He was not offered an internship.

Lesson learned: know the game *and* the business.

In an interview with a sports team or league, you may include a *brief* reference to your knowledge of the team/league from a fan's perspective, but don't spend too much time on this and don't come across as a goo-goo eyed fan. For example, you can casually mention that you attended a specific game to see so-and-so's 500th point or something subtle of that nature. Any fan references should be included as a quick mention only, or not at all. Employers don't look favorably upon interns who want to work for their organization because they seem awe-struck. Let's drive this point home with a quick quiz.

Imagine you're interviewing with The Kraft Group and Tom Brady and Roger Kraft happen to walk by. An appropriate, professional reaction is to:

a. Fall down on your knees and bow repeatedly as Tom walks by.
b. Salute as Tom and Roger walk by, but make it unclear specifically which of the two you are saluting.
c. Whip your phone out of your pocket and beg your interviewer to take a picture of you with Tom.
d. Nod your head in passing and say "good-morning" as Tom and Roger walk by. Stifle all impulses to bow, salute, or take a selfie.

If you answered anything other than response d), you may want to pursue a different field.

Employers need competent employees who understand their business. As a sport management major, it's assumed that you're passionate about sports; however, most employers will tell you that this isn't a requirement for a job with a team. Knowing your particular position and being able to effectively handle all of the position's responsibilities is a requirement. At the same time, be smart about this. You wouldn't, for example, tell the NY Yankees that you're a die-hard Boston Red Sox fan in the middle of an interview for an internship - at least, not if you want the position.

The point of conducting your research and becoming as knowledgeable as possible about all aspects of the organization, the position, and the competition is to best prepare responses to interviewing questions you may anticipate. This will make you appear prepared and competent, and it will also increase your confidence.

The key to doing this well is to actually prepare responses to the usual interview questions, not wing your responses on the spot. Some responses will need to be impromptu because you didn't anticipate the question, but many can be prepared for ahead of time. Preparing responses may take many forms. I strongly suggest (and will require of you as an assignment) that you take the time to write out responses to typical interviewing questions. This allows you a resource from which you can prepare and rehearse prior to each interview. You should be mindful of threading your research on the organization and the position into your responses (we'll discuss examples in class), so you ensure the employer realizes how prepared you are.

At the conclusion of an interview, employers will typically ask a candidate if she/he has any questions. As we'll discuss further later, it's absolutely necessary that you take the opportunity to ask questions. Candidates who don't ask questions are often perceived as being not interested or not assertive. This is also an excellent time to demonstrate how much you know about the organization by asking carefully planned questions. Some example questions are included later in this chapter.

Different Types of Interviews: One-on-One, In-Person Interviews

When feasible, many employers will ask you to their place of business to conduct your interview. Sometimes, a phone or video conference screening or preliminary interview will take place; other times, the in-person interview may be your first (and possibly only) formal interview.

In-person interviews are typically the most preferred type of interview by both employer and candidate. For employers, they're preferred because they most aptly illustrate a candidate's personality. For candidates, there's comfort in being able to see your interviewer's facial expressions while you're responding to a question. If you have the opportunity to interview in person, or via phone or video conferencing, do all you can to make the in-person interview happen. If you can't swing the travel expense, a video-conferencing interview is still preferable to a phone interview as it's easier to make a strong impression and it can be more comfortable and personal.

The next section will focus on the in-person interview. Other interviewing contexts will be discussed later.

Prepare Your Interview Materials
After you've thoroughly researched the organization and the position to which you've applied, you should start to prepare for the day of your interview. Your goal in every interview is to best sell you and your skills/experiences for the specific position for which you are interviewing. You do this by reviewing the job posting and what you have learned of the position, and identifying the necessary skills and/or experiences needed in this position. Then, determine which of your experiences you can discuss to illustrate that you have the necessary skills. While responding to questions, you want to demonstrate that you are the most *qualified, competent, and likable* candidate for the job.

Consider bringing samples of your work to better illustrate your past accomplishments and relevant skills. These additional materials may help separate you from the other candidates being considered.

Assemble a Hard-Copy Portfolio of Your Relevant Work

The materials you include in your portfolio will be dictated by the position to which you have applied. If the position requires that you write news releases and update the company's webpage, you may want to bring the news release you'll write for this class, and examples of any graphic design or web work you've done. If the position is a marketing position and you'll be doing any marketing or promotions, you could bring copies of work from relevant courses in which you may have done product pitches or created events. PowerPoint slides, informative/persuasive business reports, relevant research papers, web design work, flyers/brochures, etc., are all different examples from your coursework that may demonstrate relevant skills.

If you have work you can show the employer from previous internships, bring that with you as well. Keep in mind that former employers may not allow you to share work you did while employed by them. You should always ask for permission before doing so.

While you will be creating an electronic portfolio at the end of this course, I still recommend bringing hard copies of your work to your interviews. The act of putting a hard copy in an employer's hand makes you appear like you came ready to sell yourself – like you're serious about the job. A hard copy is also convenient for the employer as they can browse through it right then while speaking with you and associate your name with your face and your work.

Bring Multiple Copies of Your Resume, References & Cards

In addition to a portfolio of your relevant written and/or design work, you should bring multiple copies of your resume, references, and business card to the interview. Don't assume that an employer will have your resume in front of her/him the day of your interview. In fact, more times than not it seems they don't and will expect you to provide them with one. You'll want to offer them a copy before the interview begins. It's also common for employers to conduct panel interviews where two or more people will interview you at the same time (one former student was interviewed by ten people at once). All of the panel participants will expect you to give them copies of your resume *before* the interview begins.

Bring 15 to 20 copies of your resume to every interview. Invest in a nice, professional portfolio/folder to keep your materials organized and you'll appear professional and prepared.

You should also have multiple copies of your references ready. Remember, anyone listed on your reference list should have given you permission to list them ahead of time. It's acceptable to print your references on the back of your resume when handing someone a hard copy during an interview. You may then paper clip a copy of your business card to the upper corner of the resume. Have additional copies of your business card ready in case you meet additional employees the day of your interview. You may not need to offer each employee a resume if they're not spending much time with you or actually participating in the interview; however, it's appropriate to be able to offer them a business card, and even better to exchange business cards, so that you can make connections with as many people as possible in the organization.

For the sake of printing hard copies of your resume and references, it's nice to invest in quality, heavier weight cardstock.

Plan Your Attire and Travel Plans

Professional Attire

It's rarely ever inappropriate to wear a suit to an interview. Spend some time researching the culture of the organization and somewhat cater your attire to their culture. Keep in mid, however, even if it's acceptable to dress high-end business casual on a daily basis once hired, it's still appropriate to put on your business suit for the interview. The only time I might suggest not wearing a suit is if the organization is very casual, like jeans and a t-shirt casual. In this case, you'd probably be okay as a man wearing a polo and khakis, or the same level of formality for a woman. Remember, it's appropriate for you to dress more formally and professionally as the interviewee than the full-time employees may dress.

Suggested professional interviewing attire includes:

Men

Navy blue, grey, and black are typical colors for business suits. A white shirt and a somewhat colorful tie are recommended. Colored shirts are not recommended. They invoke memories of senior dances, not professional interviews. Don't go overboard on your tie, but don't underestimate the power of a tie. A unique, yet professional tie could help differentiate you in appearance from other suited candidates. Red is a power color; blue is considered a trustworthy color. A pop of seasonal color is also appropriate.

Also, remember to put on trouser socks, not your athletic socks. Your socks should match your trouser color and your shoes should match your belt. Remember to shine your shoes - scuffed shoes can completely ruin the appearance of an otherwise sharp suit. Make sure your suit fits properly and appears well tailored and ironed. Be well groomed. One agency employer told me he doesn't like men to even have facial hair.

Women

We have more options. A pant suit or skirted suit are appropriate as long as the length of your skirt is conservative. Please invest in a full suit, not just a skirt or pants and a top. Nothing looks as authoritative and credible as a full, matching suit complete with business jacket. If you're looking for a skirted suit, a professional pencil skirt will never go out of style. It should still reach almost to your knee when you're seated. As is true for men, navy blue, grey, and black are appropriate business suit colors. You may also opt for a colorful shirt beneath your jacket. A pop of color is pleasing and helps bring out your personality.

If you're prone to fidgeting, tie your hair back and don't wear any jewelry that may prove distracting. Be minimal and well groomed. Wear comfortable shoes, though this doesn't mean they have to be flats. Personally, I think heels appear professional, and I prefer to be at, or as close to, eye level with men as possible. When wearing heels, a two-inch heel is appropriate, stilettos don't belong in most offices. I still oblige the rules of my grandmother, my style icon, who always appeared as if she just stepped out of Vogue. Open toed shoes don't belong with professional attire or formal evening wear, and hosiery should be worn in the office.

Both Men and Women
If you've purchased new clothing and/or new shoes for your interview, wear them and walk around before your interview to ensure they're comfortable.

Again, once you get the job some of these attire rules may relax a bit, but until then, you can't go wrong by being well tailored and conservative. Once you get the job, keep in mind that many employers have some kind of dress code. This may include suit, shirt or tie colors, heel heights, level of formality, etc.

Regardless, and not surprisingly, research shows that the more professionally dressed and well-groomed candidates are hired and promoted up the corporate ladder faster than their sloppy-looking competition. It pays to invest in some nice pieces and to "dress for the job you want, not the job you have."

On-Time is Considered Late, Be a Little Early
Before the day of your interview, map out your destination and take a practice drive to make sure you know how to get there. Know what

your parking situation will be so you're prepared with cash or coins for meters if necessary. Remember to factor in time to walk from a parking structure to the building. Be a few minutes early, not on time. This will give you time to relax, breathe, and focus.

Once you arrive at the location of the interview, consider everything that happens from that point on as part of the interview, meaning you should be on your absolute best professional behavior with everyone you encounter. You never know who in the organization knows whom or when the employer may be putting you in what seems like an otherwise, non-purposeful situation completely on purpose to observe your behavior.

Make a Positive & Professional First Impression

When you first arrive at your interview, it's likely you'll introduce yourself and check in with an administrative assistant and then sit and wait for your interviewer(s). If you find yourself waiting near other people, employees or other candidates, mingle and socialize. Get off of your phone. The employer may be watching to see if you're social and outgoing, or completely lost in your own texting world. Be courteous and friendly to everyone you meet. This is standard respectful behavior, but you also never know when the security guard or front desk admin is married to your interviewer. It's also likely that the employer may be hiring more than one intern, so the other interviewees may not be competition for long, they may soon be your colleagues. You can use your wait as an opportunity to build further connections.

Eventually, your interviewer will come to get you for the interview. As she/he approaches you, don't wait for them to reach you before you stand up. If you're sitting, stand up as the employer gets close to you and throw your hand out to initiate a handshake. Introduce yourself with a firm handshake, strong eye contact, and give your full name, first and last, so that the employer associates your name with your face. If you're then taken into a room with more employees who will be interviewing you (such as a panel interview) or you meet other people in the office during your interview, introduce yourself to everyone with a smile, and the same strong eye contact and firm handshake. Again, don't wait for them to go for the shake first, stick your hand out there. This shows you're professionally assertive, outgoing, and confident, which gives the impression that you're also competent. As you enter the room where the interview will take place, wait to be invited to take a seat, or wait for your interviewer(s) to sit down first before you do. Of course, if this becomes awkward and it's clear that they expect you to sit down, go ahead and do so.

Use Strong Nonverbal, Verbal, & Oral Skills

In an interview your verbal responses obviously matter, so you should pay attention to your words and the examples/content of your responses. In addition, your delivery of this information is extremely important. In other words, those SM 101 skills really do matter. During your interview, speak clearly and with solid projection, as this exudes confidence and competence. Before answering questions, make sure you pause so that you appear to be thinking. If you open your mouth and respond immediately, you'll come across as being too rehearsed – and if you aren't rehearsed and you answer before thinking, it's not going to go well. You want to appear natural, but prepared. Speak clearly and at an appropriate speed, remember to pause and breathe. If you need to stall while thinking, I suggest calmly reaching for your water and taking a sip while you prepare your next response.

Be mindful of your nonverbal skills as well: eye contact, posture, head movement, feet position, and hand and arm gestures. You want to use strong eye contact so that you appear comfortable and professionally assertive, though looking away occasionally to think is also appropriate. You may want to lean in slightly while the interviewer is speaking so that you appear engaged. Then, sit up tall and strong, use solid posture as you respond to questions so that you appear "big" and sure of yourself. Your hand and arm gestures should be natural to you, but be sure not to fidget. Sit with your legs in a comfortable, non-fidgety position. It's acceptable to cross your legs (men & women) but do not let the bottom of your foot point at your interviewer. Most of the time, a desk or table will separate you from your interviewer and this will not be an issue. If there isn't a desk or table separating the two of you, be aware of personal space and the position of your legs. Practicing your seated posture ahead of time is very helpful.

You should participate in a mock interview (or better yet, a few mock interviews) prior to an actual interview, so that you can get feedback on your responses, as well as your verbal delivery. You'll want to remove verbal fillers (e.g.: uh, um, like, you know, okay, etc.) from your delivery and sound as natural and conversational as possible. Remember that solid projection exudes confidence. A mock interviewer will also make you aware of any non-purposeful gestures you may be using. Pushing your hair back, pulling on your sleeves, playing with your papers or pen, are all gestures that you may be doing that may be distracting to the interviewer or make you appear anxious or unsure of yourself, which is not the image you want to project during an interview.

You can schedule a mock interview with an advisor at the Michigan Career Center. Sport Management alumni will also make themselves available at some point during the academic year to conduct mock interviews. Be on the lookout for an email from the Kinesiology OUSA announcing this opportunity. In addition, you could request that one of your parents' colleagues or another professional contact conduct a mock interview with you. It can be very beneficial to engage in a mock interview with a professional you know to be a trustworthy advisor, but whom you don't know very well. This will simulate more of an actual, real-world interview scenario. Mock interviews can take place via phone, video conferencing, or in-person. You're advised to participate in all types as you may find yourself in all of these situations during just one organization's interviewing process.

Different Types of Interviews: In-Person Group Interviews

Group interviews are popular because they allow employers to maximize their time by interviewing multiple candidates at once while also directly and immediately comparing candidates to one another. Many of my former students have participated in group interviews for internships and full-time positions with organizations like professional teams, the NCAA, IMG and Octagon. Group interviews may involve three candidates being interviewed over dinner or even twelve candidates being interviewed in a large conference room.

Typically, in a group interview, there'll be more than one candidate and more than one interviewer. In most group interviews, it seems like three to six interviewers from the company take turns asking questions. Interviewing by yourself with one interviewer induces anxiety; for most students, interviewing in the midst of your competition induces even more. There are multiple variables to consider in this setting in order to stand out. You want to be memorable, seem competent and professional, and also present yourself like a team player, someone with whom your employers would like to work.

Interviewing with Multiple Interviewers

If possible, before your group interview begins, introduce yourself and shake hands with each individual interviewer. It's best to do this before you even sit down; handshakes should be made while standing. Make note of each interviewer's name, and offer each a copy of your resume.

As you respond to questions, try to use the question asker's name in your response. This adds a personal effect and makes you seem likable. Make eye contact with the person who asked you the question as you begin your response, and then open your eye contact to all of the interviewers. If one interviewer asks you a question and your response relates to something you said previously when responding to another interviewer's question, feel free to say, "*As I mentioned when*

Sam asked me about my role in student government...." Referring to each individual interviewer as many times as possible in the interview is going to make you seem very personable. Of course, there is a line you don't want to cross; too many personal name references will make you seem creepy.

As the interview concludes, shake hands with each interviewer on your way out, thank each for her/his time, and ask for business cards. Send follow-up, thank-you emails, snail mail cards, or both, the next business day to each interviewer. Try to include something specific from the interview in your thank you message to remind the interviewer of you and further your likability.

Interviewing in a Group Setting with other Candidates
When employers interview more than one candidate at once, they're typically trying to save time, and also compare you to your competition. They may also be using the group setting to gauge your personality and teamwork skills. Are you a good listener? Do you interrupt others? Do you readily engage while also being respectful?

It's important that you consider all aspects of this setting and appear like a professional, team player. You don't want to appear obnoxious, rude, or negative by interrupting or putting down another candidate's response or experience.

Before the interview even begins, be mindful of your setting. If you're in a waiting area with other candidates, it's likely that the employers are somehow observing you. You should not sit alone like an introvert with your headphones on and stare at your phone. First of all, your cell phone has no place being out or on during an interview. Second, you want to appear personable and likable, so use this opportunity to mingle while also assessing your competition. Engage in conversation with other candidates - look open, friendly, outgoing, and sociable. It's also likely that the employer will be hiring more than one person, so one or more of the candidates may someday be a colleague.

Once the interview begins, the interviewers may ask questions directly to a specific individual; or they may ask each candidate to take turns responding (the around-the-table method); or they may ask open questions and wait to see who chimes in first. Be personable and engaged with other candidates' responses. Look attentive as others respond, nod along with their responses, laugh if something is funny, etc. You may also refer to another candidate by name as you respond if something is similar; for example, *"Like Sarah, I also worked for IMG last summer, though I worked specifically in contracts. My experience there involved…"* This shows that you were listening and you're respectful of others accomplishments. Don't mention another candidate more than once in your response and be sure that you're talking about yourself with a lot of "I" statements to indicate your experiences, skills, and past internship responsibilities.

If the interviewer approaches the interview as a free-for-all by asking a question and waiting to see who responds first, choose your words and timing wisely. You want to answer first sometimes, but not always. You want to listen to other candidates as much as you speak, but not more than you speak. Do not interrupt others. If you cannot respond first, wait for another candidate to conclude her/his response before you begin yours. Be polite, but be active in the interview. Remember, this may very well be strategic by the employer. They may be looking for an outgoing, personable employee who will work well and get along well with diverse others in the company, but who is also comfortable speaking up and making herself/himself heard.

Different Types of Interviews: Phone Interviews

It's common for employers, especially those located far away, to conduct a preliminary phone screenings or the first round of an interview via phone. Phone interviews can save you some money in travel costs and dry-cleaning, but they're also tricky. You should still prepare by going through this guide and conducting at least one mock interview. I think the best preparation for a phone interview is to conduct the mock interview also via phone. Your mock interviewer will be able to give you specific feedback on your phone skills and responses, and you will gain comfort with the situation.

When you're scheduling the phone interview, confirm the time of the call and whether the employer will call you (the usual) or if you should call her/him. If the employer is in another time zone, also confirm the time zone for the time of the call. I once had a student interviewing via phone with Nike (located in Beaverton, OR) and, fortunately, she had the foresight to realize the day before the interview that she wasn't certain if her interview was scheduled for 1PM EST or 1PM PST. She called her interviewer to clarify and found that her interview was scheduled for 1PM PST or 10AM EST. Can you imagine missing an interview with Nike because you didn't think to clarify the time? Also, keep in mind that in the real world, 10AM means 10AM, not 10:10AM. That's a very unique "Michigan time" that in the rest of the world is called being late.

Plan for your phone interview by finding a quiet place to take the call where you won't be disturbed. If you're in your room or apartment/house, let your roommates know that you'll be on a phone interview. Some of my students have used quiet rooms in the library or study rooms in various campus buildings. Fire up your laptop to the company's home page, have your written responses to the sample questions later in this chapter in front of you, and a glass of water available. Set up any additional resources you think might be helpful.

Set aside more time than your interviewer told you to expect for the interview. If the interviewer didn't give you an idea of how much time to expect, plan for 90 minutes to two full hours. Phone interviews can vary greatly in length, particularly dependent on where in the interviewing process they're taking place. Initial phone screenings may be shorter, perhaps only 20 minutes. Second or third round interviews via phone may last from 30 minutes to two full hours.

If you're using your cell phone for the interview, which is typically the case, ask the interviewer what she/he would like to do if you should lose service. Should you call them back or vice versa? Like face-to-face interviews, your interviewer will probably start with some easy get-to-know-you questions. As the interview progresses and the questions get more challenging, don't feel rushed to answer. A pause on the phone can seem much longer than a pause in person, but it's still completely acceptable for you to pause briefly and think before you begin responding to a question. You might want to say, "Let me think about that," so it's clear you heard the question and need a brief pause to gather your thoughts. On the flip side, don't be concerned if your interviewer pauses at times. She/he is probably making notes. Speak clearly so that your interviewer can hear you comfortably. Projection exudes confidence and competence.

As the interview concludes, ask your interviewer for her/his e-mail to send a thank-you and ask her/him what the next step will be. Sometimes, a successful phone interview is followed by an in-person interview, and other times the phone interview is the only interview. My former student who I mentioned earlier had all of her Nike interviews – four in total – via phone.

Different Types of Interviews: Video Conference Interviews

Recently, more of my students have been asked to conduct interviews via Skype or some other form of video conferencing. These interviews have been for full-time positions, internships, and graduate assistantships with schools outside of Michigan. As with all types of interviews, you should prepare for a video interview by researching the company/position, preparing for typical questions, and participating in a mock interview; in this case a video conferencing mock interview would be best.

As with a phone interview, set yourself up for your Skype interview in a quiet place where you won't be disturbed. Be sure to choose a location where you'll have good Internet access. At the beginning of your interview, establish how you'll get back in touch with the interviewer should technology fail (Do you call them back or will they call you back?).

Unlike a phone interview, a video interview has the added component of your visual presentation. This can be to your advantage as it allows you to sell yourself through visuals as well as through your verbal responses. Take advantage of this and stage your scene. Determine how much of your background will be visible during the call and fill this area with subtle, relevant objects. If you're interviewing for a marketing internship, you might strategically place your marketing textbook in the background. If the position is away from home and involves possible travel, you might place a few of your vacation photos in the background to show you're open to new places and well traveled. An equally important consideration is what the interviewer shouldn't see; for example, you should probably move your adidas apparel from sight during your Nike interview. Think about your setting, strategize, and plan. At the very least, your area should appear tidy and free of anything that doesn't portray a professional image.

Finally, while this may be a video interview, you should still dress the part. One of my former students was complimented on his suit during a Skype interview for a graduate assistantship. The interviewer commented that he was impressed my student had gone through the effort to suit up for a Skype interview. While I'm sure this alone did not get him that coveted graduate assistantship (which he did get in the end – full room and board and a stipend to pursue his Master's in Sport Management), it did establish a positive and professional first impression.

Concluding Your Interview and Following Up

As your interview comes near to the end, your interviewer will most likely ask you if you have any questions. You are never allowed to say, "No." Consider this my rule that will follow you to all of your interviews. You must asking questions. Doing so makes you seem interested and also allows you to strategically ask about things you learned of during your research. In other words, you can continue to sell yourself as a top candidate, one who is intelligent and well informed, by asking the right questions.

The final section of this chapter includes sample questions that you may ask an employer.

Upon concluding your interview, shake your interviewer's hand and thank her/him for her/his time while making strong eye contact. If it hasn't already been covered, it's appropriate for you to ask what the next steps in the interviewing process will be. Finally, if you haven't already done so, ask for a business card to ensure you have the interviewer's contact information to send your thank you, follow-up email.

Sending a thank-you email and/or snail mail card is a key step to any interview. In addition to being a professional courtesy, it could also separate you from other candidates. Most employers have indicated that e-mail messages are considered sufficient. You should send an email to each person with whom you interviewed, not just one to human resources. Vary your message; don't send the same copied and pasted message to all of your interviewers from the same organization. Your interviewers will meet to discuss you at some point and I've heard from more than a few employers that your thank you message is part of their evaluation.

Your thank you message should thank your interviewer for her/his time and then mention something specific you enjoyed discussing during your interview. You include this second part to personalize your message and to make sure your interviewer remembers you. It's possible they interviewed many candidates for this position in a short period of time. Conclude by reiterating your interest in the position and include your contact information.

While thank-you emails may be acceptable, a snail-mail, hand-written card can make a bigger impact. My preference is to send both. If timed correctly, your email will get there first and your snail mail card will arrive a couple of days after. The employer will be reminded of what a strong candidate you are - twice.

Sample Thank You Message:

Dear Ms. Peterson,

Thank you for considering me for your sponsorship and events internship. I enjoyed meeting with you and learning more about the interns' roles in planning the summer kick-off series of events. As we discussed, I am confident my previous experience planning and implementing events as a marketing intern for Michigan Athletics will make me a valuable addition to your team of interns. I look forward to the opportunity to work with you and the intern team to make this summer's events successful.

Sincerely,

Abe Froman
555-555-5555
abefroman@ferris.com

Send your thank you email and snail mail card within 24 hours of your interview. I like the email to go out the next business day. If you happened to interview on a Friday, wait until Monday afternoon to send your email so it doesn't get lost in the craze of Monday morning.

Preparing for Different Types of Interview Questions

Your goal in every interview is to persuade your interviewer(s) that you're the most qualified and competent candidate for the position. You also need to come across as likable, someone your interview wants to see everyday around the water cooler. Being qualified and competent doesn't necessarily mean you've performed the exact same tasks required in this position in the past. Having the skills to perform these tasks, and the ability to learn quickly and develop new skills and knowledge, is a must, particularly for internships.

An interview is a "sell" situation, not an "inform" situation. To best sell your skills, you must know what skills are needed to effectively perform the position at hand. As discussed earlier, you do this by researching the company and the position's responsibilities. Check out the organization's website and the job posting, and talk to a previous intern, a current or former employee, or someone in HR. Then, carefully prepare your interview responses so that you mention the position's desired skills in each answer. Don't go in there and simply regurgitate information from your resume. The interview is your opportunity to expand on your resume by discussing your experiences in detail to best illustrate your qualifications and skills. You must appear confident and competent and nonverbal skills will matter just as much as your verbal responses.

While you do need to answer the direct questions you're asked by your interviewer, you can strategically work in additional "sell" information by thinking and preparing ahead of time. *How do you want to be perceived? How do you want to brand yourself? What are your best qualities? What are your strengths? What can you add to this position? What can you add to the organization?* The interviewer may come right out and directly ask you these questions, but then again, they may not. Be prepared to work your qualifications into your responses.

Most employers come to an interview with specific questions they think will help them determine whether or not a candidate has the skills necessary to fulfill the responsibilities of the open position. Assume, for example, an employer is searching for a candidate who possesses problem-solving skills. The employer may ask scenario-style questions to determine the candidate's ability to solve problems, like asking the candidate how she/he would deal with certain types of situations. *Tell me about a time you were working on a project and things didn't go as planned. Have you ever worked on a project and encountered difficulties in the design or implementation? Tell me about at time you worked with a difficult person – how did you handle it?* These questions all ask about scenarios that involve problem-solving skills. When an interviewer asks you questions that require you to respond by describing a situation you encountered, it's referred to as behavioral interviewing. This is a very common practice in interviewing as it allows employer to get to know more about you than a straight, direct answer would allow. For you, the candidate, it provides an opportunity to answer the question while working in more relevant skills. More on behavioral interviewing, and the S.T.A.R. method of responding, is provided later in this chapter.

When preparing for a behavioral interview, start by determining the skills necessary to succeed in the position for which you're interviewing. Then, choose examples from your most relevant past experiences to work into your responses. Choose different experiences rather than relying on only one. Even if you have one past experience that is clearly more related, it's best to show a more comprehensive view of yourself. The examples you choose may come from your education, previous paid work, unpaid internship, leadership or volunteer experiences.

The more recent the examples you include the better. Again, the positions themselves don't need to be similar to the one for which you're interviewing (though it's great if they are), but the situations you encountered must allow you to illustrate relevant skills. You'll want to be ready to discuss experiences in which you can demonstrate successful completion of projects or application of skills, though some interviewers will specifically ask you to recall negative situations. Be prepared to discuss situations in which you encountered difficult working situations, conflict, or adversity. In the case of discussing challenging or "negative" situations, it's important that your wording remain positions, you don't insult or criticize people you worked with previously (stick to the facts), and end your responses with positive outcomes. Your goal is to illustrate your ability to work through challenges.

Responses to behavioral interviewing questions can be much more involved and longer to deliver than direct responses. It's important to prepare ahead of time so you present a well-organized, clear answer and you don't get off on a tangent. You'll begin by describing a situation in which you experienced the situation in question. Next, you'll explain the actions you took to handle the situation. Finally, you'll conclude with the outcomes or results of your actions. These types of responses involve many "I" statements and should be delivered with effective verbal and nonverbal skills.

Responding to behavioral interviewing questions in this way is often referred to as applying the STAR Method.

STAR Method

When employing the STAR method, you'll begin by describing your example/situation in detail, including the task or goal that you were supposed to accomplish. Next, explain the action(s) you took in the situation. If you worked in a team to accomplish your goal, indicate this, but focus mainly on your contributions to the project. Your responses should include a lot of "I" statements to ensure that you're speaking in active voice, in a confident and action-oriented manner. Your story should have a beginning, middle, and end. Finally, explain the results of your action(s). Your response should conclude with the positive results that you achieved.

Following this order, the STAR method is broken down as follows:

> *Situation or Task*: describe the situation or task and your goal(s), include specific details

> *Action*: describe the action(s) you took and keep the focus on you by using "I" statements

> *Result*: describe the outcome, your accomplishments, and success; end with positive results

Below are two examples to illustrate responses following the STAR Method:

Question 1:

Tell me about a time you had to plan an event and you encountered major challenges that impeded your ability to succeed?

One of our SM alum was asked this question in an interview for an NCAA post-grad internship during the Spring of 2012.

Response 1

First, the *situation/task* is described:

As an intern with the Michigan Athletic Department last fall, I was given the task of planning a promotional event for the Michigan men's soccer team. My goal was to increase fan attendance, specifically student attendance at the game. The date of my promotional event fell on a league competition game with a team that was not a strong rivalry team, which made my event that much more challenging to plan.

Note: this situation was strategically chosen because the position with the NCAA was in their championships division and involved event planning and promotions.

Second, the *actions* that were taken are discussed:

I began my planning process by brainstorming possible themes and events. I decided to do a Halloween-themed event because the game fell on the weekend before Halloween. We had found in past events that students are attracted by give-aways, as well as fun themes and contests. The events that have been most successful at Michigan have all involved desirable give-away items.

I decided to hold a contest at my game for the best dressed Michigan fan. I also wanted to give away gift cards to local eateries and businesses. In addition, I designed a t-shirt to give away to fans; the t-shirt was printed with the name of the team and a block 'M' dressed up as a bat.

Note: I would include a graphic of your t-shirt design in your portfolio to bring to this interview.

After I planned my theme and events, I began contacting local businesses to seek sponsorship of the event. I asked local apparel stores and popular eateries for gift card donations and donations towards the cost of the t-shirts. In return, based on the amount of their donation, sponsors either received their logo printed on the back of the promotional t-shirts and/or their logo printed in the game program.

I encountered some adversity on the day of the actual game. I arrived at work five hours before the 2pm kick off to get everything ready and to set up the promotional materials at the field. Once I arrived at work, my phone began to ring and my staff started to cancel on me. One had gotten sick, one had his car break down, and two others called off with various excuses for their absences. By an hour before the gates were opening for fans to enter the stadium, I was down half of my staff and I had to reorganize my remaining staffs' assignments. I decided that instead of three staff, we only needed two staff on the entrance to manage ticket sales and fan entry. Instead of two staff standing near the main stairway into the bleachers, I assigned one staff member to that position to answer questions from fans and direct them to their seats. Then, I assigned two staff to manage the half-time costume contest rather than the original four that I had planned. I spent my time mainly rotating through my staff to ensure they were managing their stations well. I communicated with all staff via walkie-talkie to assist them when I wasn't present.

Third, the *results* are discussed:

> *Through careful planning and creative and persuasive pitches via phone and in-person visits to local businesses, I was able to successfully raise over $750 in gift cards and enough to cover the purchase and printing of the Halloween-themed t-shirts. Those were a big hit with the crowd. My marketing of the event through flyers, email blasts, and social media was successful in attracting the highest fan attendance that season to any soccer game - men's or women's. In addition, the assistant athletic director supervising me complimented me on my quick thinking and ability to revise my plan on the day of the game to ensure that all ran smoothly. She also told me that my business plan for the event was to become the blueprint for future promotional events.*

Question 2

Describe a time you had to collaborate on a project and one of your group members was difficult to get along with?

This is a very popular question that students have reported being asked in many interviews.

Response 2

First, the *situation/task* is explained:

> *Last semester, I took a sport management course titled, Consumer Behavior. In this course we studied target demographics of consumers and their buying behaviors.*

Note: This example was specifically chosen because the position required marketing and consumer research. The example involves a class rather than a previous job; however, this may be wise if the position to which you are applying involves marketing, promotions, community relations, or any responsibilities that require knowledge of target demographic groups. You can draw many examples from your relevant coursework, allowing you to demonstrate both your skills and your course knowledge (particularly useful if you don't have relevant work experience in the desired area).

> *My group was assigned the task of developing a new marketing and promotional campaign for the Ann Arbor YMCA. We immediately encountered some difficulties when one of our group members started missing deadlines during the early stages of the project. At this point, it wasn't a big deal because I was able to complete his tasks for him with the help of another group member; however, I knew that we couldn't continue to have one of our group members miss deadlines and manage to complete this project well- and I don't believe in doing anything less than the highest quality work. If I'm working on something, I strive to complete it to the best of my abilities with a close attention to detail.*

Next, the *actions* taken are explained:

> *So, I decided to speak with my group member right after I noticed that this may be an ongoing problem. I emailed him and asked him to meet with me half an hour before our next scheduled group meeting, so that he and I could speak before the rest of our group members arrived. I started our conversation by explaining to him that I was concerned that he hadn't met the first two deadlines that the group had set because I cared about this project and wanted to complete it to the best of our abilities, and score an A. I asked him if there was anything he needed help with that was causing him to miss our deadlines.*

> *It turns out that he wasn't proficient at research. So, I offered to meet with him that week in the library to go over some of the library resources with him and walk him through the main on-line resources*

and databases that we use for our research. This meeting went very well and after it he scheduled a meeting with one of the librarians to seek more help. I think he just needed to be pointed in the right direction and motivated a bit to get things done.

Third, the *results* are discussed:

My group's final written report and presentation resulted in an A and compliments from our professor for the breadth of our research, as well as my group's ability to work well together and present a coherent, concise, and professional final presentation. Two employees from the Ann Arbor YMCA also attended our final presentation. They were so impressed with our project that they asked us to implement two of our proposed promotional events at the YMCA last winter. Two of my group members were able to do this. I wasn't able to commit my time as I was already committed to my position with the men's basketball team as a team manager; however, my group member who I had spoken to early on in the project did take the YMCA up on the offer. Our ideas successfully attracted greater participation and local support for our YMCA.

Notice the detail in both of these responses. The interviewees in these examples carefully prepared and rehearsed their responses in advance. During their interviews, they described their situations by including relevant detail and action words, and they concluded by describing positive results. These are not one or two sentence responses. These responses took time to prepare and time to deliver. This is the level of detail required in a strong STAR method response.

Strategically prepare your examples based on the position's responsibilities. Remember, you want to describe examples that answer the questions; however, these types of questions allow you the opportunity to also choose the most relevant examples to illustrate your diverse skills and best sell you as a competent candidate. Be sure to use "I" in your responses, so you are responding in active voice, which delivers more confidently than passive voice. If a situation you wish to explain didn't end with a positive result, be honest and explain what happened, and then conclude by explaining what you took away from the event, what you learned and will apply to achieve positive results the next time you face a similar situation.

These are only two sample behavior-based questions. Many of the questions that appear later in this chapter are also behavior based and should be responded to by applying the STAR method.

Sample Interviewing Questions

The next section includes a selection of fairly typical interviewing questions. These are meant to act as a guide as you begin your interviewing preparation process. Following most questions is a brief description of what the employer may be looking for in your response.

1.   *Tell me about yourself.*

This is typically one of the first interviewing questions and its response is referred to as your "elevator pitch," which was discussed previously in our chapter on networking. While this is somewhat of a rapport question, allowing you to describe yourself and establish a personal rapport with the interviewer, you need to fight the urge to fall into a deep recital of your childhood. Instead, think about the five top things this potential employer should know about you. This could include academic or work experiences, or specific traits or skills.

This question is often asked first, because it allows you and the interviewer to become comfortable in the situation as she/he begins to learn more about you. It's a key opportunity for you to begin your "sell" by including specific experiences or skills in your response that begin to set you up as a competent candidate for the specific position for which you are interviewing. This response should be delivered conversationally with confident language and tone and strong eye contact. Consider including one unique aspect of yourself to make yourself a bit more personable and also memorable (you would be surprised how many employers want to talk about broomball).

We'll discuss elevator pitches further in class and you'll have the opportunity to rehearse and receive feedback.

2.   *What do you see yourself doing five years from now? (Other variations of this question: What are your career goals? What are your long term plans?)*

The interviewer wants to hear that you see yourself succeeding *in this industry* in five years, possibly in a higher position with more responsibility, etc. If you're interviewing for a position with a marketing firm, but you hope to one day attend a graduate program to obtain your doctorate degree in philosophy, this isn't a time to be completely honest. An employer may be looking to hire an intern with the thought that this intern may one day be a full-time employee. For this reason, an intern is an investment of time and training. You want the employer to think of you in this context.

3.   *What do you like to do in your spare time?*

This is a personal, get-to-know-you question and you can go ahead and be honest - to a degree. If you really spend all of your free time watching *Sports Center* and reruns of *Friends*, then you have a problem. Your interviewer is trying to get to know you and they want to know that you do something productive in your spare time. Playing sports, reading, and spending time with your family are all good answers. If you engage in activities that are relevant to the position, be sure to mention them; for example, if you are interviewing for an internship with *Sports Center*, then watching *Sports Center* everyday is actually a strength and should be mentioned.

Also, remember that people want to work with people they like and we tend to like people who are like us. So, if you find a common interest with your interviewer, go with it and spend some time on a tangent; for example, if you see a picture on your interviewer's desk in which she/he is skiing and you like skiing in your spare time, then include this in your response.

4.   *If I asked three of your friends to each describe you differently what would they say?*

One of my past students was asked this question in an interview, except the interviewer asked her to tell him three different things six different friends would say about her. Do the math. That's eighteen different things! She said it took her about fifteen minutes just to respond. Part of the interviewer's intention in asking you this question is to put you on the spot and see how you react. Also, hearing how those close to you would describe you allows the employer to learn something about the kind of person you are through the type of friends you keep. Invariably in your answer, your interviewer will learn how you know these people, in what context, and a bit about your relationships.

Personalize your response by stating each friend's name, how you know them, and what they would say about you with a quick reason for why they would describe you this way. This can actually be a time to drop in strategic "sell" information; for example, you might choose two friends with whom you worked in a previous job. This allows you to include additional information about your experiences and skills. Keep your adjectives job relevant; in other words, being "friendly, kind, and loyal" is great, but being "ambitious, dedicated, and a hard worker" is great – and job relevant.

5.   *If you could change one thing about the past four years what would it be and why?*
The interviewer is looking for you to thoughtfully reflect on your past four years and comment on something you wished you had done differently or earlier. Think about including something that is job relevant to demonstrate experiences you are engaging in currently that

have prepared you for the specific position for which you are interviewing; for example, if you were interviewing for an internship with the Detroit Downtown Development Authority, your response might be:

> *I would have liked to have gotten involved in research earlier. I didn't hear about all of the opportunities available in Sport Management and elsewhere on campus until my sophomore year, which is why I didn't start pursuing any until then. Once I started working with Professor Rosentraub my junior year, I quickly realized how beneficial the experience was going to be. I learned a great deal about urban planning and the role of stadium construction in reshaping the landscape of cities. I'll be able to apply the knowledge I gained through this experience and the research and data analysis skills I developed directly to this position with your organization.*

6.   *What achievements are you most proud of? (Apply STAR Method)*

This is your chance to brag. Go ahead and do it by including a position-relevant example; for example, if you are interviewing for a marketing internship, then the "A" you received on your capstone project in your marketing class is an excellent example. You should follow the STAR Method when responding by explaining the project, the work you completed, and the outcome. Perhaps also include that your "A" was a major achievement as the professor was a notoriously hard grader.

Keep in mind that this is an easy response to change based on the position to which you have applied and the organization in which you would work. Your examples should always be as position-relevant as possible. Every response is your opportunity to "sell" you and your qualifications.

7.   *How do you make yourself indispensable to a company?* (Another variation: *What can you bring to this job?*) *(Can Apply STAR Method)*
This response should include your specific skills, those that are most relevant to the position. Also, include mention of your soft skills, such as your excellent communication skills, ability to work independently or in a group, professionalism, etc. As you describe your skills, apply them to various examples to make them seem authentic. It's always stronger to explain how you have applied your skills than it is to simply list your skills. Examples also make you more memorable.

8.   *What is your greatest strength? (Can Apply STAR Method)*
This is a prime time to work in one of your wonderful anecdotes to explain your strength(s). In other words, relate your strength by describing how you've used it to your advantage in a professional or academic situation in the past. You may need to change or tweak this answer from interview to interview as you make yourself seem the most appealing for different positions. For example, in an interview for

an internship involving sales, you may want to stress your excellent verbal and oral communication skills; while in an interview for an events-planning position, you may want to stress your ability to work under pressure and meet deadlines.

9.   *What is your greatest weakness?*

No one loves this question, except interviewers. I think I have been asked this question in every interview I have ever done. On the flip side, I think I've also asked it in every interview I've ever conducted. This is not a trick question. The interviewer is looking for you to demonstrate knowledge of yourself and your ability to recognize and work with your weaknesses; however, they don't want to hear about how absolutely horrible you are about getting up on time for classes (even if this is the total truth).

You want to be honest in this response, but not so honest that you'll raise a red flag by listing a weakness that could be detrimental to your ability to do the job. Stay away from the standard "negatively-positive" responses like, "I take on too much" or "I'm obsessive about details." Anytime an interviewee responded to me with something like one of these responses, I would press them for another weakness.

While you may be able to spin a negative into a positive in your response, do so with honesty and subtlety, and again, refrain from raising any red flags by including something too negative; for example:

> *In the past, I had difficulty working late into the evening hours on assignments and getting up for my 8am classes. This was definitely a problem for me my freshman year. I took on too many activities and did not account for how challenging my academic courses were going to be, so I didn't schedule myself enough time to complete assignments. This was a great learning experience as by sophomore year I prioritized my activities and dropped a couple of them to allow more room in my schedule to focus on my academics and also get involved in a research study on professional teams' corporate social responsibility with Professor Heinze. I've learned that I do better academically when I schedule my time carefully, get my work done before it gets too late, and factor in enough time for a good night's sleep. I like to wake up early so I feel like I've made the most of my day.*

10.   *Tell me about a time when your course load was heavy. How did you complete all your work? (Apply STAR Method)*

The interviewer is looking for you to demonstrate your abilities, your time management skills, and your ability to coherently explain your actions. In this case, they want to know that you're prepared to handle a stressful on-the-job workload. You may also strategically drop in more "sell" information by naming relevant courses you have taken, or even relevant course projects that contributed to your heavy course load. Refrain from calling classes by their numbers, like "SM 217," because employers won't know what you're talking about. Name classes by their actual titles or describe them in a relevant way if the title itself is a mouthful (SM 111 can simply be described as a "history and sociology of sport course").

As you describe your time management skills, add a little detail. You may want to say that you learned the value of using your Google Calendar and making yourself adhere to mini deadlines. Again, describing these skills in the context of an example that includes actual courses and/or course projects will strengthen your response and make it authentic and memorable.

11.   *Tell me about a time when you had to accomplish a task with someone who was particularly difficult to get along with. (Apply STAR Method)*
As discussed earlier, this is actually a behavioral interview question and you should respond by applying the STAR Method. As you respond, keep your answer positive and refrain from speaking too negatively or in any kind of personal way about the difficult person in question. In general, you should avoid bashing anyone (colleague or former employer) in an interview and keep the language positive. Focus on describing the person's actions that were negative, not the person. Negativity in a response establishes negative energy in the

interview and you don't want to be remembered by the employer with any kind of negativity.

Most importantly, tell the employer how you dealt with this person, the actions you took to rectify the situation and handle the conflict. The employer wants to hear that you have developed mature and professional interpersonal skills and that you can handle dealing with difficult people. Remember to include the final results, which ideally were positive. It they weren't positive, include what you learned and how you'll apply it to keep such difficult situations from arising in the future, or handle them if they do.

12.   *How do you accept direction and at the same time maintain a critical stance regarding your ideas and values? (Apply STAR Method)*
This is a tricky question that involves walking a fine line. You want to show that you're willing to take direction and listen to authority, but that you also hold your own ideas and values to be important. An anecdote would be a great way to answer this question, but if you don't have a relevant story to share, you can use a hypothetical situation. Have something prepared either way to demonstrate that you're comfortable sharing your ideas and presenting them to an authority figure (educator, employer, advisor, etc.). Again, it's

important to include that whether or not the authority accepted and incorporated your ideas, you still followed her/his instructions.

13.   *What are some examples of activities and surroundings that motivate you?*

This is another answer that may change depending on the position and the employer. For example, if you're applying for a marketing or public relations job that involves constantly working with other people, work this into your answer as something you enjoy doing:

> *I enjoy working with people who are motivated. I love dynamic situations and challenges that allow me to use my communication skills and leadership skills; for example, as a hostess at Pizzeria Maria in my hometown, I enjoyed working busy Friday nights and double shifts on Saturdays. There was always a wait list and it was my job to greet the customers, manage the wait list, answer the phone and schedule call-ahead seatings, and also offer light refreshments to our diners while they waited. It was a lot to juggle. My manager would often commend me on my ability to engage in small talk with those waiting while also managing the seating chart and answering the phone. I knew our regular customers by name, and they also knew my name, allowing me to give them a better, more personalized dining experience. I was so good at managing all of these tasks and communicating with the diners and our wait staff that my manager soon had me training every new host he hired.*

14.   *Tell me how you handled an ethical dilemma. (Apply STAR Method)*

This will most likely be class related for many of you. Perhaps you had a team member who you knew plagiarized part of a team paper or a research partner who broke some equipment and then threw it away without informing the professor. Ethical behavior is important to employers as evidenced in the many questions I receive on the topic from employers when I'm giving students job recommendations.

Think about an anecdote you can share to illustrate your strong sense of right and wrong and your professional assertiveness, or ability to deal with uncomfortable situations. It's important to demonstrate that you'll act ethically yourself and that you'll take action when necessary to ensure that your peers or colleagues are doing so as well.

15.   *Tell me about a time when you had to resolve a problem with no rules or guidelines in place. (Apply STAR Method)*

Like many of these questions, this one would be a tough one to answer on the spot without having considered your response ahead of time. Basically, your interviewer is looking for you to show that you can recognize situations and problems and that you're willing to act when necessary. They don't want to hear that you sat back and watched as something went wrong. Your response should follow the STAR Method and may include an example from an academic or professional experience. The more relevant the example is to the responsibilities of the job to which you are applying the better.

16.   *What would you do if you won the lottery?*

You never know when these seemingly irrelevant questions are going to pop up. Sometimes they're asked simply because your interviewer has spent the entire morning conducting interviews and now they're bored. Other times the interviewer wants to gauge how well you think on your feet and respond impromptuly, which often relays more of your personality. While the odds of actually ever winning the lottery are slim, please don't tell your interviewer that you'd immediately quit your job.

This question is a great example of a question that may not seem at all job relevant – and really is not. It's a "fun" question, an opportunity for you to demonstrate some of your personality and make yourself memorable and likable to your interviewer. If you're funny, apply a little humor. If your interviewer already told you she enjoys traveling, go on a trip somewhere exotic. If you're interviewing with the NY Yankees, perhaps purchase season tickets or go on a tour of every ballpark in America.

17.   *What can you tell me about this job?*

Do not fail this one! Trust me, 99.9% of the time it will come up. If it doesn't, it's only because the interviewer is waiting for you to demonstrate your knowledge of the position and the organization without being prompted. Please do your research ahead of time and don't be afraid to tell the employer where you've gotten your information. Tell her/him you spent time perusing the company website, or you read an article about their recent growth in Forbes, or that you spoke with Mary from Human Resources during an informational interview you initiated. This shows initiative, drive, and a desire for the position.

Also, remember that each response should "sell" you and your skills, so follow up what you know about the position and the organization with a strong statement reiterating why you're the best candidate to fill the position.

18.   *What is your definition of success?*

There really is not one right answer to this question. Your response should be personal and involve career achievement or achieving quality work, or possibly even working for the specific organization with whom you are interviewing (though the position and your career don't have to be the focus of your response). You may also include mention of happiness, family, etc.

The content of this answer is important, though I believe the delivery to be of even greater importance. This response should be delivered with confidence and authority with no long "thinking pause" before responding. I like to think of it as ending with a very well emphasized period so that you appear as someone who knows what they want out of life. This has the effect of making you appear confident and competent.

19.   *Describe the process you go through to make a decision. (Apply STAR Method)*

If this is a position that involves making important decisions, this question is obviously that much more important to the success of your interview. Let the interviewer know that you make well-informed decisions only after gathering information to consider different options; this allows you to weigh all of the pros and cons of the different options to make a well educated, level-headed decision. This response is strongest when the STAR Method is applied. Try to incorporate an example that is relevant in some way to the position.

20.   *If you were asked to plan a (insert your name)-themed promotional day at (name of ball park or venue at which you are interviewing), what would you plan?*

The Toledo Mud Hens and the Michigan Athletic Department have asked this question of my students in past interviews and I'm sure it's come up elsewhere as well. The interviewer is looking for you to show your creativity while also getting a feel for your personality. As you prepare this response, think strategically and include information to demonstrate your knowledge of the organization, such as the team's target demographic fan base, previously successful promotional events, etc. Your promotional event should be focused on the team's target demographic of fans and also include their current sponsors.

Then, think about what you want the interviewer to know about you, something relevant, memorable, and something you can describe while also explaining how and why your event will be a success.

21.   *If you were a type of cheese, what type of cheese would you be?* Crazy, I know, but it does happen. I was actually asked this question in an interview for a full-time consulting position. It's another one intended to throw you off your guard and let the interviewer see how well you can think on your feet. One of my previous students was asked what cereal she would be and another former student was asked which superhero he would be.

If you're asked a seemingly random question, do not panic. Pause and gather your thoughts quickly, and then go with something. This obviously is not a very serious question. Use humor (if you're funny) or simply pick a response and go with it. I was Swiss cheese, *"because I find it to be the most interesting of cheeses. It's versatile. It can be lacey with little holes or traditional with big holes. It tastes great in omelets, sandwiches, salads, or on a cracker, so it keeps surprising you and you never tire of it."* The interviewer actually cracked a smile and I was later extended a job offer (I'm not saying it was because of the amazingness of this response, but I also don't think it hurt).

22.   *You may tell the occasional lie in this position. Are you okay with that?*

A few former students have been asked this question in both internship interviews and interviews for full-time positions. If you say yes, you have admitted to being a liar. I think the only correct way to respond is to say, "No," and assume that the interviewer was checking your ethics. If they were serious about you needing to lie, maybe you don't want this job anyway.

23.   *What makes you angry?*

If your spidey sense is going off, good, it should be. Your interviewer may be trying to bait you to see if they can get some insight into what makes you tick or they may be testing your character to see if you come across as an aggressive person. Anger has no business in the workplace, so the first thing you should do as you respond is soften the language. Then, use an example of something that may "bother" you, but which you have learned to handle; for example:

> *Well, I pride myself in getting along with all sorts of people, but to be honest, it does bother me a little when people are not punctual. I don't mean being late one time because you had car trouble or something, I mean consistent tardiness. I think that shows either a lack of planning or perhaps lack of respect for the work or the event. I pride myself in being punctual and I appreciate when other people are as well.*

As an alternative, if you have established a rapport with the interviewer, you're funny, and they seem to be digging your humor, you can try a little humor in this answer by responding with something completely irrelevant to the position and work:

> *I get annoyed when my roommate puts the orange juice container away empty. It's an ongoing joke in our apartment that she puts things away empty all the time. Fortunately, she has lots of other redeeming qualities.*

24.   *Are you more creative or practical? (Can apply STAR Method)*

This question is worded so that the interviewee responds with either one or the other. A few years ago, I was attending a panel presentation of sport industry executives and a woman from IMG said that she always looked for interviewees to respond with *"both creative and practical."* I think the key is to then apply an example to support that you're both to authenticate the response and make it memorable. Your example should illustrate your practicality and your creativity through an example that is as relevant to the position for which you're interviewing as possible.

25.   *Sell me that pen.*

Variations of this question have been asked of my former students in numerous interviews, particularly those involving any form of sales. Some students have been given an object to pitch and a few minutes to prepare; other students have been put on the spot and expected to respond immediately (after taking a "thinking pause" to gather your thoughts and mentally plot a course of action).

One of my former students was told the week before his interview with a financial company that he would have to give a 15-minute sales presentation. He was asked to choose the product and design a presentation complete with PowerPoint slides. He strategically chose a product to pitch that fit the organization's products, prepared his presentation, and scheduled meetings with faculty in the SM Program to ask for feedback. In the end, his efforts paid off as he was extended a job offer.

26.   *What are three things I should know about you?*

Be ready to present your three most powerful strengths that make you the best candidate for this particular job. Remember, these attributes may change from one interview to the next depending on the position. I think this response delivers best when you state your skills/traits with confidence in one statement. You could also apply examples to illustrate your skills, though if the interview has been going well and you've already discussed a number of your relevant examples, I would deliver this one as a one-liner to exude confidence.

27.   *If you were any position on the basketball team, which would you be and why?*

One of my former students was asked this question while interviewing for an internship with a team in the WNBA. She responded with "Power Forward" and then explained how the skills necessary to play this position matched her skills, which not coincidentally were skills required to succeed in the internship position for which she was interviewing.

28.   *What question would you least like me to ask you?*

This may be a trick question in that if you actually respond with a question you don't want to be asked, you can expect that the interviewer will ask you that question. Be prepared to answer any question you suggest. This may be a good time to insert some humor – if you're funny and the interviewer appears to be responding well to your humor. Gauge your use of humor carefully; too much can make you seem like you're not serious about the job.

29.   *What is your definition of professionalism?*

Two of my students were asked this question during interviews for internships during the 2013-2014 academic year. Your response should run the gamut of professionalism from behaving respectfully, being on time and dressing appropriately, to representing the organization's ideals during business and non-business hours and in all use of the organization's image, including social media. Think about the organization's goals and mission statement, as well as the responsibilities of the position to which you have applied. Cater your answer to cover anything you think would be relevant.

30.   *Why should I choose you?*

When this question has been asked in student interviews in the past, it's typically been near the end as the interview is winding down. If you're concluding the interview, then you just went through your resume and your qualifications with your interviewer. Now you can end with a strong final statement. Your statement may reference your most relevant strengths again or an experience/skill that separates you and makes you more qualified than other candidates. Simply stating, "because I am the best person for the job and I want this job more than other candidates" is not enough. Give the employer a specific reason to remember you and choose you.

31.   *What salary do you require?*

It's not likely that you'll be asked this question during an internship interview. It's more likely this question may be asked in a final interview for a full-time position, at which time you should have researched the average salary for this type of position accounting for the cost of living in the geographic area in which you would be working.

There are a few websites that include information on starting salaries adjusted for cost of living by geographic area. Alternatively, or in addition to these websites, you may choose to conduct an informational interview with a professional in the field, such as a U-M or Sport Management alum.

When you respond to this question during the interview, it's appropriate to let the employer know how you have determined your desired staring salary. Typically, you give a $5,000 range when asking for a salary (e.g.: between $45,000 and $50,000). You may want to follow this up with another remark supporting why you're worth this salary.

32.   *If we did offer you the job, how would you react?*

Your potential employer wants to hear that you want the job, you're enthusiastic about it, and you would take it if offered; however, I also think it's best to be honest, or at least within the realm of honesty. If you're also waiting on another offer from a different employer, you may want to tell the current employer that you're very excited about the prospect of working with them and you would appreciate a few days to consider your living arrangements (or travel arrangements, finances, etc, something legitimate) before making a decision. They may give you the time, but they may not.

If you find yourself with one job offer to which you must respond in a couple of days, but your first choice of internships is still pending, you may call the employer who you're waiting on and politely let them know you have received an offer and then ask if there's any way they will make a decision in the next two days (or however much time you have to make a decision for the other employer). Also, let them know that they're your first choice. In the past, this has gone both ways for my students. Some have had the employers get back to them with offers (or a response to let them know they would not be offered an internship) and other employers have told them that they couldn't make a decision in the desired time frame.

If you're in the latter situation, you'll need to make a decision: take the offer on the table OR hold out for your first choice. *I do not recommend taking the first offer and then reneging on it should the other offer come through.* The sport industry is small and well connected and you don't want the reputation of being someone who backs out on commitments.

Questions For You to Ask the Employer

As mentioned earlier, most interviewers will ask you if you have any questions for them before they conclude the interview. You are not allowed to say "no." Use this opportunity to strategically ask questions to illustrate your knowledge of the organization. This may include questions about recent, current, or future happenings in the organization (stay away from controversial topics). It's okay for you to bring these questions written on paper and it's also okay, and a good idea, for you to write down the answers given to you by your interviewer.

Sample Questions for You to Ask Your Interviewer

1. *What can you tell me about the day-to-day responsibilities of this position?*

2. *How has this job been performed in the past?*

If the position's responsibilities haven't been discussed in detail before or during the interview, you should ask these questions so that you can be sure you're interested in performing the job duties. These questions also show the employer that you're serious about working in the position. You can also turn these questions into another "sell" opportunity. Even though you asked the question, you may follow up the interviewer's answer by reiterating your interest and qualifications that make you the best candidate to fill this position.

3. *What happened to the person who held this job before?*

If you're applying for a full-time position, you may want to ask what happened to the person previously in the position so you're aware of any problems or past history associated with this position; for instance, was your predecessor fired or was she/he promoted? Is this a temporary position or a brand-new one? The answer will tell you about your supervisor's expectations and possibly your opportunity for career growth at this organization.

4. *Why did you choose to work here? What do you enjoy most about working here?*

As much as an interview is intended for the employer to assess you, it's also your opportunity to further assess an organization to make sure you think it's the right fit for you. Although you may like this company from what you've heard or read of them, you need to find out what an insider has to say about working there. Who better to ask than your interviewer? This also forces the interviewer to step out of their official corporate role and answer personally as an employee and potential coworker. It can help establish a personal rapport between you and the interviewer. People like to talk about themselves.

5. *What is the first project the person you hire must attend to?*

This is another question you may ask to show your interest and also increase your knowledge of the position. Again, if applicable, you may want to follow up by reiterating your strengths/skills that will allow you to tackle the project immediately and achieve quality results.

6. *I understand that you have recently expanded your ticket plans to include an all-you-can-eat ticket option? (Or a similarly current-event- type question.)*

This is a sample question that illustrates specific, current happenings in the organization. The idea is to ask a question that shows you're interested in learning about the specific position and the organization, and that you've already done research and are familiar with their current operations. This shows that you're serious about the position. It also has a subtle complimentary effect in that people enjoy talking about themselves and typically respond favorably when others show an interest in them. By asking about recent happenings of the organization, you allow the interviewer to spend some time talking about what she/he does, furthering your rapport and making you more likeable.

7. *What's our next step?*

This is your closing question if the interviewer has not already gone over it. Be aware that many employers will give you an expected timeline of when you can expect to hear from them with a decision, though most employers will take longer to actually get back to you. After going over the next steps, ask for your interviewer's business card so that you may send your follow-up, thank you note. Extend your hand for one final, strong handshake, thank the interviewer for her/his time, and express that you look forward to working with them soon – *working with* as opposed to *hearing from* - it doesn't hurt to be confident.

Remember to send your thank-you email (and possibly snail mail card) the next business day. Then, as you wait to hear from the employer, you may drop them an email once every other week or so to update them on any new developments in your work or education, or to send them an article or news that you found interesting and relevant to the position. You don't have to wait in silence. You can stay actively engaged with the employer to keep your name and your interview fresh in their mind. This is a fine line of communication, as you want to be actively in communication, but not annoyingly so.

Final Interviewing Notes

As you interview for positions, please send me any interesting, challenging, or surprising questions that you're asked. If you send them to me, I'll add them to this guide to assist future Sport Management students as they prepare for their interviews. Even if no "new" interview questions are asked of you, I always appreciate hearing how you're doing with your career searches. Updates are appreciated after graduation, too!

Remember, we have numerous resources on campus to help you get started in your internship search, prepare your application materials, establish and promote your professional brand, network, and prepare to interview successfully. Make use of these resources early and often and you'll set yourself up for internship and career success.

In Summary:

1. An interview is a "sell" situation, not an "inform" situation. You need to present yourself as qualified, competent, and likable.

2. Prepare for each interview by researching the position's responsibilities, the organization, your interviewer(s), and the organization's competition. Include your research in your responses to show you're knowledgeable and interested.

3. Assemble a hard-copy portfolio to bring to the interview. Include any relevant samples of your work (written or design).

4. Invest in a professional folder to bring to interviews to hold about 15 resumes/reference lists and your business cards.

5. Plan your attire and your trip to ensure a professional appearance and timely arrival.

6. Be courteous and respectful of everyone you encounter during your interview, and engage with other candidates.

7. Don't be a fan. When interviewing for a team or league, put aside your love (or dislike), it's irrelevant. Present yourself as a business professional.

8. Prepare for each interview by planning and rehearsing your responses to typical interview questions. When possible, apply the STAR Method to respond to behavioral interviewing questions. Participate in mock interviews ahead of time.

9. Send a thank-you note within 24 hours of your interview.

Chapter 7

Making the Most of your Internship Experience

Chapter 7   Making the Most of Your Internship

Once you've received an internship offer and accepted it, spend some time celebrating (and congrats to you!), and then sit down and get back out the laptop because it's time to do some more planning. Before you show up on day one, there are a number of things you should know in order to make the best first impression and set yourself up for a successful experience.

The purpose of an internship is to develop your knowledge of various areas of the industry and build your professional skills. Ideally, you learn as much as possible about your position and the organization before your experience concludes, and you make a positive impression on your supervisor and any other employees/interns with whom you work. You may want to ask for a reference letter before you leave. The sport industry is also small and well networked and it's likely you'll cross paths again with some of your coworkers, or they may be contacted in the future to provide a reference of you. It's common for potential employers to contact previous employers if they know someone in the organization, regardless of whether or not you listed them as a reference. If you leave your internship employer and your coworkers thinking of you as a smart, professional, hard-working intern, they'll be able to provide an excellent recommendation for you.

Before You Arrive for Day 1

Before you arrive for your first day of work, there are a number of things you should know. If you haven't been asked to attend a formal orientation, you can call your supervisor or a human resources representation and ask about the following:

Attire

Is there a dress code? Is the office business professional or business casual? We'll discuss the difference between the two further in class. Basically, business professional is a suit while business casual is pants/pencil skirt and a nice top. *Business casual **is not** leggings, jeans, or sneakers.* Those are just straight casual. Remember the advice given earlier, your appearance may affect how likely you are to get a full-time offer, or be promoted once hired. As an intern, you should strive to dress on par with the best-dressed employee in the office. Those who look more professional appear more authoritative and credible. This includes your clothes, your shoes, and your grooming. Be conservative and professional.

Time

What time are you expected to arrive and what time may you leave? Keep in mind that you never want to be the last person in for the day or the first person to leave. If your supervisor asks that you arrive by 9am, I'd suggest being there by 8:30am. If she/he says you may leave by 5pm, I'd plan to stay until at least 5:30pm or later. Even if you aren't expected to clock out, your supervisor and others will notice.

There may very well be days when you've completed all of your tasks. Find something else to do. Ask your supervisor if you can assist with anything else. If nothing is offered, there's always something to clean or restock. Of course, ask before touching any supplies or inventory that are out of your responsibilities. You may also find some literature on the organization or its competition to read (not on your cell phone, they'll think you're surfing). You may also ask to speak with other employees and conduct informational interviews with those in other departments to learn more about the organization as a whole.

Office Culture

It may take a little while for you to feel comfortable in the office and get a feel for the culture of the organization. Is it normal for people to leave early on Fridays? Is it acceptable to eat at your desk? Do people generally gather around the coffee pot in the morning and talk for a bit before getting to work? You'll figure out much of this on your own, but I still recommend asking ahead of time, *"Is there anything I should know about the office culture?"*

Once You Arrive for Your Internship

Once you begin your internship, there are a number of things you can do to make the most of your experience, and make the most positive lasting impression on your supervisor.

Use Good Office Etiquette

Applying good office etiquette really means having good manors. If something isn't yours in the fridge, don't eat it. If you leave food in there for a few days, dispose of it. If you make a mess, clean it. If you empty the coffee pot, make more coffee. If you use the last paper in the copy machine, restock more paper. These are just some of the obvious good office etiquette rules.

Some other, less obvious rules include knocking on people's office doors or cubby walls, even when open, and waiting to be invited in before entering. If you hear that someone is on the phone, don't stand there and listen to them. Come back in a few minutes. Don't enter your supervisor's office and expect to be able to have a ten-minute conversation with her/him at any time. If you have questions or material to go over that will require more than a couple of quick minutes, schedule an appointment with her/him. Don't "reply all" to an email when it isn't necessary and don't forward or include people on sensitive emails without your supervisor's approval. When in doubt, ask questions.

Finally, one of the most important office etiquette rules, *do not be on your phone during meetings or even at your desk during business time.* If for some reason, your phone is integral to your job and in participating in a meeting, then of course, be on it. This is rarely ever the case. Even if your supervisor is on her/his phone during meetings, you should not be. They have a full-time job and they're the boss. You're an intern. Behave better.

Make It a Learning Experience

Learn as much as you can while you're at your internship. Be open to feedback from your supervisor and others. Ask questions when you need clarification, or when you don't know why something is being done. One of the best comments I receive from employers on our students' performance as interns is that they came ready to learn and seemed interested and ambitious. You may think you need to act like you know everything in order to appear credible. This is not the case. Most employers expect that you'll need to be brought up to speed on many things. Even if you're working in your third marketing internship, the two previous organizations may have operated very differently. Your current supervisor will expect you to have questions.

Of course, you don't want to ask too many questions. When you can, search for the answers on your own. Also, recognize that other interns or the administrative assistant may be able to answer your questions; not all need to be answer by your supervisor.

Your supervisor will be a busy person. She/he may set up formal times to meet with you to discuss your work; however, if this doesn't happen, you should seek opportunities to receive feedback. Once you've completed a task or major assignment, schedule an appointment with your supervisor and come to the meeting with questions prepared. Your intention is to find out what went well and if there's anything you can improve upon. It's important that you be open to this feedback – some of it may be critical. Most supervisors offer critical feedback in order to help you improve, so hear what she/he is saying.

Stay in communication with your supervisor. A summer internship can go by very quickly. In addition to scheduled feedback meetings, I suggest writing your supervisor a summary of your completed tasks each Friday before leaving for the day. Include your prioritized plans for the coming week. If your supervisor is out of the office often, this may be the best way for the two of you to communicate and for your supervisor to stay apprised of your work.

Work Well with Your Fellow Interns

Most of my students return from internships to tell me that they had a wonderful experience, learned a lot, and had a great time. Often, you'll work closely with a team of interns. This can be a great experience as you have a peer group at work of similar age. This group may also become a social group outside of work.

It's to your benefit to work well with the other interns. In the immediate setting, they're your peers and you'll be completing work together. Your supervisor will expect you to behave well and solve problems, or challenges you may face working together, on your own. Your supervisor will not want to referee, so if you find yourself working with an intern who you dislike, deal with it. You need to respect those you work with and learn to work together to complete tasks. It's not required that you like one another.

In the future, your fellow interns may prove to be helpful contacts to help you connect with an industry professional, or perhaps even to help you get hired. You never know when you'll cross paths with colleagues in the future.

If your intern group becomes a social group, be mindful of your actions while at work and outside of work. Don't let any bad behaviors of other interns influence you to behave badly. If they all start leaving work early, you shouldn't. If they all go out late to party and come to work in less-than-ideal condition the next day, you shouldn't. Remember, you represent yourself, Michigan, and the Sport Management Program. You should conduct yourself professionally at all times to maintain our excellent reputation with employers.

Network While on the Job

Use your time at your internship to network and build professional relationships. You may have one direct supervisor to whom you report. You shouldn't ask to work with others without your direct supervisor's consent. In the event that you're completing your work ahead of deadlines, ask your supervisor if she/he has more work for you. If not, you may ask if it's acceptable for you to ask others for work. This may be allowed and it may not. I've known of supervisors to say no, simply so you are on call whenever they may need you. In the event that she/he says yes, this could be an opportunity for you to connect with other employees and build relationships.

You can connect without working for or with someone as well. In your free time, you may ask to conduct informational interviews with other employees in the organization. This can be a great way to build professional relationships and also learn about other positions. Ask about their backgrounds, experiences, and their work responsibilities. *You might ask what skills are necessary to do their job? What are the desired qualifications in a new hire in their area? Do they have any recommendations for you of other experiences you should look into to build your skills?* These informational interviews can take place in the office, or outside over coffee or lunch. I strongly suggest getting to know as many people across the organization as possible while you're interning. It's the best time to make connections while you can meet in person.

Ask for a Reference Letter and Resume Review

About two weeks prior to completing your internship, ask your supervisor to write you a recommendation letter. As discussed earlier, it should be written on organization letterhead and a digital copy is best. It's also very helpful to update your resume with this internship experience prior to leaving, so that you may ask your supervisor, and/or other employees with whom you've connected, to review your resume bulleted descriptions.

Seek Help and Advice if Things Go Unexpectedly or Badly

Most of our students have wonderful experiences at their internships. They learn a great deal, establish strong connections, and receive positive and encouraging feedback from their supervisors.

Some of our students have okay experiences, which typically means they learned a little, but not as much as they would have liked. Perhaps they spent a lot of time on menial tasks. This is fairly typical in a first internship.

On very rare occasions, a few of our students have found themselves in bad situations. On one occasion, a student found himself working in an environment that could be perceived as harassing, for a supervisor who was berating and condescending. On another occasion, a student began her internship only to find her responsibilities were nothing like she was expecting, and not at all what she had agreed to. In another situation, one of our students experienced sexual harassment.

This is not meant to alarm you. Again, most of you are going to have wonderful (or at least not awful) experiences. In the event that you find yourself in an unpleasant situation, or worse, you must seek help. You're always welcome to call us during the academic year or over the summer if you need advice. I'm available via email or cell. You may also call your faculty mentor or OUSA academic advisor. It's important that you reach out to someone and seek advice on how to handle the situation.

After Your Internship Concludes

Once you've completed your internship, spend some time reflecting on your experience. If you haven't been logging your experience, record the tasks and projects you completed. It's surprising how quickly you'll forget all of the things you did. Make a record of your work immediately upon concluding your internship, so you have a detailed summary of your work. You'll need this to update your resume and LinkedIn profile, and write future cover letters. Again, it's ideal if you update your resume and ask your supervisor to review your bulleted descriptions before you complete the internship. In the event this didn't happen, update your resume immediately upon completing the internship so your work is fresh in your mind.

If you registered to receive academic credits for your internship experience, complete your paperwork and final requirements and submit those prior to the posted deadline.

It's also helpful to spend a little time reflecting on how this internship relates to your academic coursework and your future career plans. *Did you apply any concepts from your coursework to your internship? Did you find you lacked a skillset or knowledge that you could improve upon by taking a specific course? Did this internship experience affect your intended career path? What type of position/organization should you seek to intern for next in order to continue developing your professional expertise and strengthening your resume?*

Upon returning to campus after completing your internship, make an appointment with your faculty mentor or career counselor to discuss any questions or thoughts that may have come up as a result of your reflection. You may also find it helpful to talk with trusted advisors with whom you've connected via Linked In or through previous work. Having a mentor in your intended field can be extremely valuable as you continue to seek professional advice. Your internship may be an excellent time to establish such a connection.

In Summary:

1. Before arriving for your internship, talk to your supervisor or an HR representative to ask about appropriate office attire, arrival/departure times, and office culture. Dress similarly to the best-dressed employee in the office and never be the first to arrive or leave work.

2. Practice good office etiquette while interning: be polite and respectful of people's/organization's property, space, and time.

3. Stay off your cell phone during business hours (unless its needed for work.

4. Work well with your other interns. They're your colleagues now and may be in position to help you get a job in the future.

5. Represent yourself, the University of Michigan, and the Sport Management Program with excellence in all of your work and out-of-work endeavors during your internship.

6. Network and build professional connections. Do this in your free time by asking employees if you can conduct an informational interview in the office, or over coffee or lunch.

7. Seek help from your faculty mentor, academic advisor, or career counselor if you need advice during your internship.

8. Ask your supervisor for a reference letter and to review your updated resume before your internship concludes.

9. Reflect upon your internship immediately after completing it to assess how it influences your future academic and career plans.

Made in the USA
Lexington, KY
06 September 2018